DAY TRADING:

QUICK STARTERS GUIDE TO START DAY TRADING

Andrew Johnson

© 2017

Sign Up & Join <u>Andrew Johnson's Mailing List!</u>

*EXCLUSIVE UPDATES

*FREE BOOKS

*NEW REALEASE ANNOUCEMENTS BEFORE ANYONE ELSE GETS THEM

*DISCOUNTS

*GIVEAWAYS

FOR NOTIFACTIONS OF MY _NEW RELEASES_ :

Never miss my next **FREE PROMO,** my next **NEW RELEASE** or a **GIVEAWAY!**

information presented is without assurance regarding its continued validity or interim quality. Trademarks that mentioned are done without written consent and can in no way be considered an endorsement from the trademark holder.

THIS COLLECTION INCLUDES

THE FOLLOWING BOOKS:

A Beginner's Guide to Day Trading: Discover How to Be a Day Trading King

AND

Day Trading: The Ultimate Guide to Day Trading: Uncovering Day Trading Profit Making Secrets

AND

Day Trading: Strategies on How to Excel at Day Trading

TABLE OF CONTENTS

A BEGINNER'S GUIDE TO DAY TRADING:

DISCOVER HOW TO BE A DAY TRADING

KING

DESCRIPTION

Day trading is often a misunderstood investment, but it can be one of the best if you want to make money now, rather than waiting for the long term. You will work in the stock market, but instead of making a purchase and holding onto a stock for months and even years, the day trader will make purchases and sales of the same stock, all in one day. It is an exciting investment opportunity, but it is important to learn some strategies to get the most out of your investment.

Inside this guidebook, we are going to learn the steps for success in day trading. Some of the topics we will explore include:

- The basics of day trading

- The rules for success

- How to complete a key analysis to master day trading

- Further analysis on how to succeed at day trading

- Additional day trading strategies

- The best platforms for day traders

When you are ready to put your money to work with a great investment opportunity that provides you with an income each day, day trading is the answer for you. Check out this guidebook and learn everything that you need to know to get started in day trading.

INTRODUCTION

Congratulations on downloading your personal copy of *A Beginner's Guide to Day Trading: Discover How to Be a Day Trading King.* Thank you for doing so.

The following chapters will discuss some of the many things that you should know to get started with day trading. Day trading can be a great way to make money from purchasing and selling your stocks all in one day. We will discuss some of the basics of day trading, as well as many of the different strategies that you can use, such as a fundamental analysis and a technical analysis, to make sure that you see success in this investment.

There are many different options with day trading and if you work on your research ahead of time, it is easy to make a good income. Day trading has gotten a bad name because many beginners turn it into a gamble, taking on more risks than necessary and losing out on everything. But a true day trader will do the research, weigh the risks, and make decisions that limit their losses.

When you are ready to learn the different aspects of day trading and how to make this investment work, check out this guidebook and learn all about day trading for your needs.

There are plenty of books on this subject on the market, thanks again for choosing this one! Every effort was made to ensure it is full of as much useful information as possible. Please enjoy!

CHAPTER 1: THE BASICS OF DAY TRADING

Investing your money is a smart financial move to help your income grow without having to put in more hours in the office each day. There are quite a few investment options that you can choose to go with depending on your interests, amount of time available, and how much money you would like to earn. Some investors like the idea of placing their money into a retirement plan and keeping it safe there. Some investors like being in the real estate market and owning property to make their money. Investing comes in many shapes and forms and the trick is finding the option that works for you.

But an option that many investors miss out on because they simply don't know about it is working on day trading. This is a form of investing in the stock market, but rather than holding onto a stock for a few years or longer, you will make your purchases as well as your sales all in the same day. This requires a good understanding of the stock market, the trends that are going on in the economy, and understand how quickly the market can turn in just a day.

With your day trading, you will need to pick out the stocks you want to purchase, make the purchase, and then sell them by the end of the day to make a profit. There are a few different strategies that go with this and often they make just small profits per each one, but when you add these together over a few days, you are going to see some results of huge profits for you. Some traders choose to borrow money in order to take advantage of some of the smaller price movements in the market, but you should be careful with this in the beginning.

Before you make a purchase, you need to understand the market well enough to know that there will be an increase in the value of the stock during that day. While most stocks stay fairly steady over the years, slowly going up a little bit over the long term, there are quite a few fluctuations that can occur in that stock from day to day. This is where the day trader will be able to make their money. They can take the variations that occur in a stock during the day and predict where it will go before making the purchase and hopefully seeing a profit.

The main idea with day trading is that you will be able to enter the market at the beginning of the day, looking for a stock that has a low price. After a bit of research on this stock, which you have probably been doing for a bit beforehand anyway, you will expect that the price of that stock will go up by the end of the day at the latest. With the right plan in place ahead of time, you will purchase that stock at the low price and then by the end of the day sell it for a higher price to make your profit.

There are many factors that come into play concerning the amount of profit that you will make. The amount that you paid for the stock, how high the stock goes during that day, and whether you released the stock before prices started falling again will all determine how much you are able to make. When it comes to day trading, you often will not make a big profit on individual stocks because of the brevity of your trading. But when you make many trades throughout the day and do this each day, you can start to make a good income with day trading.

As a beginner, it is important to realize that day trading can be a great way to make a profit in the stock market relatively quickly, but it is also possible to lose some money in the stock market as well. This is a risky investment because the time period is so short in day trading and often this results in inconsistencies and issues with watching the trends. Over time, you will become more familiar with the charts and tables for the stock market and you will be able to make better predictions.

The next question that many beginners have is what they are able to purchase and sell in day trading. The good news, you will be able to trade in anything that you want on the stock market. Many people stick with equity stocks because of all the options that come with them, but you could branch out to other components if you wish for day trading. Even penny stocks can be useful, but most beginners stay away from this because there aren't that many buyers and sellers, which makes it hard to do the trading in one day.

One niche that is popular with day trading is currencies through Forex. This specialty will need some research and knowledge of the market, but it can work well since there is a high volatility and liquidity for these options. If you do trade in currencies, make sure that you keep updated on the various currency exchanges; just a little shift in one could cause shifts in other currencies as well.

These are a few of the niches that are popular with more experienced day traders, but as a beginner, it is best to stick with the stock market. The stock market poses the lowest risk and you will be able to pull up a lot of charts and details to help you make accurate predictions. The liquidity is also there so you shouldn't have issues with purchasing and selling the stocks that you want to trade that way and since the stock market is full of options that stay on a consistent pattern, you can really start to see which ones will work for you.

The benefits of day trading

Day trading is a great investment option that you can choose when first starting out. Whether you decide to do this on the side to learn the ropes and make your money grow, or you are looking to turn this into a full-time income, there are options for everyone who would like to get started.

The first benefit of day trading is that you will not have to worry about overnight risks. Many other stock market investments have issues with what can happen to the stock overnight. This can be especially true if you work on stocks in other countries, or ones that rely on these other countries, because a lot can change in that time. When you choose day trading, you will be able to make all of your purchases and all of the sales in one day, finishing up before you go to bed that night. As a day trader, you are not going to be concerned about what happens to the market that night. Worst case scenario, you just take a day off from trading if the market goes way south and you don't see it going back up.

Many traders like day trading because it provides them with a lot of options. You are able to pick from working on the stock market to picking options, to work on securities, and even working with different currencies if you would like. As the trader, you need to decide which market you are most comfortable working in before starting.

The options for the strategies you are able to use provide a lot of variety in day trading. Each trader has their own strategy in this game and many times more than one strategy is going to work to bring you money. It is your responsibility to learn more about the strategies, which we will discuss in more detail later, and then stick with the one you choose. As you get more familiar with a strategy, t will become easier to recognize the stocks and options that fit with it, and you will see your income grow.

If you are a trader who likes to research your options and likes to make sound decisions based on this research, day trading will be the right option for you. This means that to see success, you need to make sure you think logically about your choices, rather than letting your emotions get in the way. For those who let their emotions get in the way of their decisions, it is best to pick another option because day trading is not going to work well for you. But if you are willing to research a plan and stick with that no matter what the market does, you will come out on top.

As a day trader, you are going to appreciate the high profits you can earn in a short amount of time. Once you get into your rhythm and learn how to work with day trading, you will find that this investment can make you a lot of money in a relatively short amount of time. If you are successful, you can make your profits in just one day, much faster than you are able to do with pretty much any other investment.

What some people don't understand about day trading, which s why many of them don't get into this market, is that you actually have some control over the amount of risk that you are taking. This trading option does have some risks, but if you pick out a good strategy, learn how to keep the emotions out of it, and make sound decisions, you will find that you control a lot of your risks with this investment.

Being ready for quick decisions

In order to see success with day trading, you need to be able to work fast inside of the market. You will be making your purchases and your sales of the stock within one day. You don't get the benefit of holding onto the stocks and riding out the market for the long term like in other investments, so your decisions need to be quick. You have to recognize the daily trends and when a stock will go up and down within just a few hours, and this can be risky and tough for some people to work with.

If you are someone who likes to hold onto stocks for some time, or you aren't good at making decisions quickly, the day trading investment is not the right one for you. While you can take some time to look over the different stocks and get used to the graphs and the different aspects of your chosen stocks, you will need to be able to make the purchase and know when to let it go all in the same day. For some people, this can be too stressful to handle and they will want to pick out an option that gives them longer term results.

Personality traits for day trading

Before you decide to look at day trading, you need to make sure that you have the right personality type. There are some people who will do amazing at day trading because they are able to do research, avoid the emotions, and just make sound decisions. On the other hand, there are some people who are too emotional, can't make quick decisions, and are just not that great at working in this kind of investment. Some of the personality traits that are needed to see success in day trading include:

- Not ruled by your emotions: as a day trader, you must make sure that you are not allowing your decisions to be controlled by your emotions. If you allow the emotions to come into play, you can end up holding onto stocks that are losing you money, picking out the wrong stocks, and just doing poorly overall on your investment. You must be someone who is levelheaded before being able to work on day trading and actually see success.

- Willing to take some risks: day trading is pretty risky to get into. You are able to reduce some of the risks that you are taking, but since you are required to purchase and sell the stocks all in one day, the risk factor is going to be higher compared to some of the longer-term investments that you can work within the stock market. While long-term investments allow you to ride the ups and downs of the market, but day trading is over such a short time that you will have to be really good at guessing the trends because if they go down, it is unlikely to be enough time to go back up.

- Good at recognizing trends in the market: if you look at the charts for a particular company and you are not able to see some of the trends over time, this is not the right option for you to get into. Unless there are some big changes in the company, most stocks will have some trends that you can use to help make your decisions.

- Willing to research and read the news: It is impossible to be successful if you just pick a stock and hope it works out. Successful day traders are able to get started in this market because they research what they are doing. They are very familiar with the trends for their stock and know exactly when to make the purchases and when to sell them. They also take some time each day to read through the local, national, and even international news to see if any changes will occur in the market that could affect their stocks.

Day trading is not an investment that works for everyone. Some people will find a lot of success with this investment, and others will not be able to make it work. But if you have some of the personality traits from above, and you are sure to find that day trading is the perfect investment option for you.

Understanding your goals for day trading

Before we get into the day trading game, it is important to understand some of your goals. There are many different reasons that investors choose to go with day trading, but your reason is going to help you to make your decisions. Keep in mind that there is a level of risk that comes with day trading and depending on where you are in life, and what you would like to accomplish with day trading, you may make different decisions.

For example, if you are in your 20s and just starting out, you may be willing to take more risks. You have time left to work on your retirement or to try some of the other investment options if day trading doesn't work out for you so you will take some of the bigger risks. But, if you are in your late 50s, you may want to work on putting money on your retirement rather than losing it all so close to this time, and so the risks that you take with day trading may be lower.

Understanding where you are in life and what you would like to do with your investment will help you to decide what stocks to purchase, how much you would like to make from this investment, and much more. Either way, you still need to work on doing your research and learning about the market ahead of time to ensure you get the best results inside this investment.

Understanding how you react to different situations is also going to be important when you work on day trading. Some people are more inclined to doing well with day trading because they are able to research the options, think through their decisions, and will stick with their plans no matter what. They understand when the market is going down and won't go back up, and they know when it is time to pull out of the game, even if they are losing money. They can cut their losses, making it easier to do well later on, rather than holding onto a dying stock and losing even more money.

If you are able to stay with this kind of mindset while trading, day trading can be a great option for you to choose. But, if you are someone who is controlled by their emotions, someone who will hold onto a stock as it rises, just to see it lose money rather than stick with the plan, or someone who holds out hope that the stock will go back up rather than cutting your losses, day trading is not something that you should consider.

Day trading can be a great way to earn some money while investing in the stock market. Instead of waiting for years to get your income like traditional investing, day trading allows you a way to earn money each day. You will need to spend some time researching and coming up with a good strategy to pick the right stocks, but with some practice, you will make a good profit on your day trading endeavors.

CHAPTER 2: WHAT ARE THE RULES OF SUCCESS?

Now that we know a bit more about day trading, it is time to learn a few rules that will lead us to success. This is an exciting time, but learning the right steps to ensure success can help even the beginner to do a great job. You will find that day trading can be completely different compared to some of the other investments that you choose because all the work happens within a single day. You won't have a lot of time to ride the ups and downs of the system, so understanding the market ahead of time can make a big difference.

If you have decided that day trading is the option for you to make money from an investment, there are a couple rules that beginners can follow in order to help them to avoid mistakes and do well with this option. Some of the rules that day traders can use to actually earn money from the beginning, rather than hoping it will all work well and losing out, includes:

Understand the three E's:

The three E's of day trading include enter, exit, and escape. Before you even enter the market, you need to have a plan prepared. This plan needs to include an enter price, a price that the stock should be at before you are willing to make a purchase. Then it needs to have an exit price, or the price that the stock will reach and you will sell, no matter what happens during the rest of the day. Having an exit strategy can be helpful as well in case the price starts to drop so that you can limit your losses.

Having this plan in place will help you to make as much as possible, without missing out when the market goes back down. When you set these points, make sure that you stick with these. As a beginner, you may let your emotions get in the way of smart decisions, but if you set up this plan and stick with it, it is much easier to make money with day trading.

Wait to trade

When making your trades, you should wait to make purchases until after the market opens. There are a lot of changes that occur during the first fifteen to twenty minutes in the stock market and it is hard to predict how the market will play out. Wait for a few minutes at least and then make your purchase when things level out a little bit. Once you see that the craziness of the first few minutes fades out, you can make a purchase knowing that the trends you have studied will be in play.

It is tempting to get into the market right when it opens, but there is a lot of fluctuation that occurs here and a position that looked good at opening can quickly change. It is only fifteen minutes to wait, so why not just enjoy that cup of coffee a bit longer and then go in and do your trading after that time occurs.

Avoid the margin

As a beginner, you may be tempted to use the margin to help increase your profits in day trading. When you are using the margin, it is basically like taking out a loan from the brokerage firm. You can take out this money to pay for part of the investment or all of it, but this can lead to some big problems for the beginner. Some experts will use the margin to help them increase their potential returns, but for beginners, it is best to never spend more money than you can afford to lose. If you end up using the margin and the trade goes against you, you are going to end up losing twice as much. It is a huge risk for a beginner who is not used to the market and until you perfect your strategy if ever, you shouldn't use the margin.

When you first get started with day trading, you should stick with just using your own money to make the trades. It can be dangerous to borrow money from the brokerage firm, they are mostly offering it in the hopes of making extra money, and just use the money that you have available and are willing to lose.

The best thing you can do for day trading is to only spend money that you have readily available. This may mean that you have to start small with just a few trades or you will need to save up for a bit in order to reach this point, but it is always for the best. Betting more money than you have can make day trading into a gamble and using the margin means that you could lose out on twice as much money when it is all said and done. Protect your investment and only use the money that you are able to use.

Set up your plan for selling

Most investors are going to just think about entering in the stock market, but they forget to come up with a strategy for selling their stocks. But if you want to make a profit, you have to sell the stock at some point. Without a good strategy, you will find that you will miss out on some of the profits you could make, and you may even hold onto the stock too long and lose a lot of money in the process.

When you enter the market, determine when you would like to get out of the market. How much profit is good for you before you exit the market? It is not a good idea to ride out the market because while some people are lucky and can get out at a higher profit, many times the market turns suddenly, and you may lose out or make a lower profit. Decide what exit point you would like to meet, and then sell when you reach that point, regardless of whether the stock continues to go up or not.

Take notes along the way

As a beginner, things are going to be pretty new to you and you may need to try out a few different options before finding the path that helps you. But if you are trying out different things, working in different markets, and more, it is easy to forget what works and what doesn't over time. It is a good idea to write down some of your strategies over time so you can look back at them when needed. You will honestly learn more from your mistakes than from your successes, but this is how you grow your profit in day trading.

When you first start with day trading, make sure to purchase a small journal and then take a few notes about all of the trades that you work on. Even if t was a small trade, a trade that went really well, one that went poorly, or one that didn't really do much, it is important to write down the details. You never know when a new trade comes up and you can use the notes that you wrote down earlier to help you become successful.

Try practicing

Practicing how day trading works is a good way to gain confidence in the investment and to try out a few different strategies It can also help you to see f you are really cut out to do day trading or if you should try out a different method of investing before you lose out on a lot of money. Many brokerage firms have trial accounts that let you input your own numbers to experiment with so you can try it out.

Whether you think you need it or not, try out the trial account. Choose realistic numbers to start out with so you can see how much you would really earn or lose in day trading. For example, if you plan to put in $10,000 to start, it doesn't make much sense to experiment with $100,000 in the trial account. Take this part seriously so you can see how you would actually do when playing with real money.

Pick out reputable sources

When it comes to day trading, you want to make sure you are picking out sources that give you accurate and timely information. You have a lot riding on this information and it would be a shame to pick out the wrong stocks or sell at the wrong time because your sources were not all that great. It is important to look for how your sources will benefit from your actions. Some sources simply want you to make a purchase because it helps them make a profit, but then will dump you as soon as they sell to you. Learn how to follow some of your own judgment and you will make the right choices.

Be prepared to cut your losses

Most beginners are excited to get into the stock market and start earning money from day trading. And with some good research and picking out a good strategy, you can make profits from this option. But you also need to be ready to lose money as well. There are times when the stock that you choose isn't going to do so well, and learning how to cut your losses can make the difference between losing a little bit of money, and losing a lot of money. Some beginners are so desperate to make money in day trading that they will continue to hold onto the stock while the price keeps plummeting.

Before you purchase a stock, decide when you will exit the game. Once the stock reaches that low point, you sell, regardless of it being a loss or the potential for it to go back up later on. Yes, there is the possibility of the stock going up, but you can always repurchase and try again. But if you held on to that stock hoping the market would go back up, you could end up losing a lot of money in the process.

Learning how the day trading market works does take some time and effort. Beginners need to have a good understanding of how the market works and you should be able to pick out the right strategy that will help you to make the most profit. No matter where you are in your journey of day trading investing, make sure to follow some of these simple rules and you will see success.

Common mistakes to avoid

In addition to following some of the rules listed above, it is important to understand the common mistakes most beginners run into when they start day trading. Some of these mistakes are pretty obvious, but when you are in the trade and trying to make a profit, you may find that it is easier to make these mistakes than not. Some of the most common mistakes to avoid in day trading include:

- Lack of preparation: day trading is not a form of gambling unless you aren't prepared. You can't win in this investment simply with luck on your side. When you win, it is because you took the time to plan out your strategy and to think out your moves. Beginners need to educate themselves about day trading, look through the information that is available to them, and learn how to make informed decisions if they want to make a profit.

- Not using all the tools available: day trading does require some tools to help the trader be successful. You should consider adding many of them to your strategy to get the best results. Some of the tools that you can include are educational resources, charts and graphs, trading software, and brokers. Without some of these tools to help you out, you will find that it is hard to trade.

- Keep it small: many beginners are tempted to go big when they get into this investment. They want to make a lot of money right away. But this is not the proper way to be successful in day trading over the long term. This kind of go big attitude turns our investment into more of a gamble, which also makes it more likely that you will lose money as well. It is just fine to look for smaller profits in day trading because this helps to reduce your risks.

- Averaging down: this is a mistake that could take a small loss, and turn it into a big one that will ruin your whole account. Sometimes t is tempting to think that since a stock is considered cheap at $5, it is an even better deal when it reaches $4. But using this method means that you are basically choosing a stock that is at a losing position. It is best to not pick this stock in the first place because it is likely to go to a lower price soon, and if you already own the stock, it is time to cut your losses.

- Holding onto the stock too long: it can be hard to lose in day trading, but holding onto a stock for too long results in really big losses. If you have a plan for cutting your losses, you may still lose a little bit of money, but it helps you to look at the market logically and not hold onto a stock so long that you lose your whole portfolio.

- Avoid vengeance trading: this is a common mistake that many investors get into and it can cause you to have to leave day trading pretty quickly. With this one, you may have just lost out on $600 on one particular trade, but you will go and search for a trade that is of equal value in order to make that money back. It is always a good idea to look for new trades that will help you earn a profit, but if you are just choosing stocks because they could potentially bring that loss back to you, you will end up losing more in the long run.

Day trading is hard enough on its own. You have to balance a lot of plates and make decisions quickly in order to make the purchases and the sales all in one day. Make sure to avoid some of the common mistakes listed above to ensure you are not inadvertently costing yourself a lot of money in trades.

CHAPTER 3: A KEY ANALYSIS ON HOW TO MASTER DAY TRADING

So now that we know a bit about the basics of day trading, it is time to learn some of the strategies that you can use to help make your trades profitable. A technical analysis is one of the best strategies to use in day trading because it allows you to take many different aspects of the stock into consideration before making the purchase. Unlike some of the other strategies, the technical analysis is not going to have you look at the stock or all the fundamentals because you are really just holding onto this stock for a day or less, so these don't matter as much.

The short-term trades in day trading is what makes this a different type of investment compared to some others in the stock market. You aren't going to worry so much about how solid the company is because you are just worried about how it will behave today. If the stock ends up going downhill after today, you can always look for another option. In day trading, there are a few things that you will need to understand and watch out for to help you to pick out the right stocks including:

- Volatility: to see success, you need to see that the market is moving and that the price of your stocks is not stuck in one place. If you look at the price of the stock and see that it doesn't have fluctuations in the price, it is not a good one to invest in. Preferably, you will want to find a stock that starts out at a low price point but will go up during the day so you can increase your profits. When looking at the charts for a particular stock, you want to see it go up and down in some sort of pattern; this pattern will help you to determine when you should enter and when you should sell the stock.

- Liquidity: not only are you looking for the price of the stock to move throughout the day, you need to make sure that there is enough trading volume of the stock for it to be worth your time. Nothing is worse than getting a stock and making the investment, just to find out that no one else is interested in the stock and you are stuck with it. Look for a stock that not only has a pattern with the price point but will also provide you with enough buyers and sellers so you can leave the market when you want.

The parts of a technical analysis

To start a technical analysis, there are a few factors that will come into play to help you see success. Learning these parts and understanding how they work will help you to pick the right stocks and earn a profit as well. The main parts of a technical analysis include:

Volatility

So the first thing we want to look for when working on a technical analysis is the volatility of the stock. You will notice when looking at the stock market that there are plenty of shares that are traded in the various markets, and these trading decisions are going to be made by investors and traders, all of which are going to try and keep their own interests in the forefront without really caring about how others do in the market.

If the prices of the stocks are moving around, this means that there are many investors who are purchasing and selling the stock. This is good news for the day trader because you have a better chance of finding options that can be profitable for you. You may notice that when big events go on with a company, the volatility of that stock will change as well and this can help you to earn more if you can make the purchase before prices go up; this is why watching the news and trends in the market can be very beneficial to you.

As a beginner, it is important to learn how to recognize the signs of volatility inside the market and see the patterns that happen. This will help you to understand when there is a lot of movement in a particular stock and can make it so you get in when the prices are low and sell when they are high.

Liquidity

When you hear the word liquidity inside the stock market, you most likely hear it when people talk about how much trading is going on with your stock. Since day traders are working on a limited amount of time to make their purchases and their sales, they don't want to end up in a situation where they aren't able to find someone to purchase their stocks later on. A market that is liquid is considered good because it provides the investor with opportunities to make some good purchases while also allowing them to find a buyer later on whether the market goes up or down.

As you get into this investment, you will start to notice that there are some markets that aren't liquid. In these markets, you will find that it is hard to purchase stocks and it is almost impossible to sell them later on, especially when you only have a few hours to do both. Without the opportunity to make purchases and sales, it is hard to make a profit in day trading so it is important to stay out of these markets altogether.

Pivot points, resistance, and support

All of these are points that you should know about to make a technical analysis. They are all mathematical equations that can take the recent performance of your chosen stock and will help you to see if they are good to work with. The first one is the pivot point and to work with this one, you will need to get information from the closing from the day before; specifically, you need to find the high, low, and the close from the previous day. Then you are able to use this formula to come up with the pivot point:

(high + low + close)/3

Remember that you are able to get this information from the previous day. Using the pivot point can be a great way to start because they reflect the different trading levels that are the most recent and when you take a look at them, you will be able to notice whether some shifts are on the way. Or example, if you notice that the stock is going higher than your pivot point, your closing is most likely going to end up higher than the previous day, as long as something drastic doesn't happen during the day. If you notice that the stock prices are lower than the pivot point, the closing will end up lower than the previous day.

Now that we understand a bit about the pivot points, you are able to use this information in order to figure out the resistance levels and the support levels. The formulas that you need to find out these points include:

S1 = (P * 2) – High

S2 = (P * 2) – (High – Low)

R1 = (P * 2) – Low

R2 = P – (High – Low)

The resistance level is basically the price that the stock will not go above for at least that day because it is too high. If a stock does go above the resistance level, this is called a breakout and usually, there was a big event that caused this to happen that the numbers would not show at all. The support level is the level that the stock will not go below, and it follows the same idea as the resistance level. In most cases, as long as external events stay the same, the stock is going to remain pretty consistent.

When trying to figure out the resistance level, you will not only need to use the formulas above, you will also need to bring out some of the charts and graphs and look at the history of your chosen stock over the past few months. For example, if you are looking at these charts and you notice that the stock never seems to go above $30, but it gets close, over that time period, this is probably your resistance level. For some reason, investors are willing to hold onto the stock until it reaches about $30, but then they sell it off. Unless some dramatic changes occur, the stock will not get above this amount, and this would be the place where you would want to sell the stock to make your profit.

This is just a part of your strategy, though. You now know where you would like to sell the stock based on the history of the stock and its resistance level, but when should you purchase the stock to get the biggest return on investment. This is where the support level will come into play.

When working on the support level, you ae looking at the point on the graph that shows how low the stock will go. When looking at the formulas that are above and the charts for the stock, you will notice that over a few months, the stock doesn't seem to go below a certain level. For some reason, other investors feel that when the stock reaches the support level, it has become a good value and they will start purchasing again. You would want to purchase the stock as close to the support level as possible to help you to make the biggest profit.

This helps you to come up with the strategy that you want to use. You will want to purchase the stock when it gets close to the support level so you can get the best deal on this stock. Then when you notice the stock is getting close to the resistance level, you will want to sell the stock before the price goes back down. Say that the support level is $10 for the stock and the resistance is $30; you would want to try to purchase the stocks for the $10 and sell them for as close to the $30 as possible, making a $20 profit on each stock in the process.

Many people like to use the technical analysis to help them make decisions on which stocks to purchase. You have some great formulas to work with and even the history of the stock to back up your decisions. You do need to keep track of the news and any shifts in the company as well because these can cause dramatic shifts in the stock that go away from the history that is in the charts, but for many stocks that remain steady, this is a great way to get started because the numbers stay pretty consistent and it is easier for beginners to get started with. It is not the only method to use, but it is pretty secure for making at least a little profit each day in day trading.

CHAPTER 4: FURTHER ANALYSIS ON HOW TO SUCCEED AT DAY TRADING

While the technical analysis is a good option for beginners to get started with, there are other options that you are able to use in order to help you to make smart decisions in day trading. The next one that we will talk about is the fundamental analysis because it will look at a few more aspects of the stock other than the up and down movements that occur on the charts. With the fundamental analysis, we are going to take a look at some of the specifics of the company rather than just what is on a chart. For example, the fundamental analysis would look at things like the revenue versus the debt, how strong the company is, brand recognition, and more about the company. It helps you to see if the company is in a good place in the market based on how the company is organized and run.

In this chapter, we are going to take a look at some of the aspects that are needed to perform a fundamental analysis. It is going to rely less on the charts and graphs that were used in the technical analysis, but t looks at some specific aspects of the company to ensure that it is being managed properly to see a return on investment.

Fundamental analysis

A fundamental analysis can be another method to help you pick the stocks that you want to trade with and even when to enter and exit the market. Some people choose to work with just a fundamental analysis and others will combine this with the technical analysis we discussed a bit earlier. When we use a fundamental analysis inside of the stock market, we are focusing on some of the underlying factors that can affect how the company runs and how it will react in the future. It is possible to use this type of analysis regardless of whether you are talking about the industry or the economy. It is often a term that can be used in order to refer to the wellbeing of the stock inside the economy, not just a look at the price movements of the stock.

There are a few questions that day traders should ask that concern the company you want to trade in when using the fundamental analysis. These questions include:

- Is the company seeing a growth in revenue?

- Is the company able to bring in some kind of profit and if they are, how much profit do they bring in.

- Can you tell if the company is in a position that is strong enough to beat out their competition, both now and in the future?

- Is there potentially any issues with the company being able to repay their debts?

- Is there any potential within with the management and are they behaving in an ethical manner?

These questions may seem simple, but they will actually require you to do some research on any company that you want to purchase stocks from. While there are a few questions that you asked above, it all boils down to one main question: is this a good company that is strong and has stock that you are able to trust?

A fundamental analysis is going to consider two different factors to help you make your decisions. First, we are going to look at the quantitative information or the information that you are able to measure out in numerical terms. Fundamental analysis will also require qualitative research, or the character or the quality of something, such as the quality of a company, rather than how big or small the company may be.

When working on your trades, you will find that quantitative information is most often used because it allows you to look at a lot of numbers. These numbers will give you insight into how the company is doing and if they are performing in a manner that can make you some money. For example, if you look at the financial statements of the business, you will be able to find the quantitative data about that company. But, if you are looking for some of the qualitative features of that same company, it is going to be a bit harder to find. This information would include things like the name recognition of the company and who runs the company, both of which can be harder to rate.

It is possible to find companies that have both high qualitative and quantitative features at the same time. For example, when we look at the Coca-Cola company, we will notice that it meets both of these categories. This company as a great financial sheet, where they are able to pay off their bills and still bring in a high revenue. In addition, this company also has a good reputation, one that people know about and trust. Even though this company does have a combination of both features, it is often not a good one to use for day trading because the stock is already close to its peak, without really reaching a low point, but it shows how both categories can come together.

It is possible to combine together the fundamental analysis with the technical analysis. There are some things that are missing from both of these analyses, but combining them together can help you to fill in the gaps and makes it easier to get the results that you want. For example, you wouldn't want to pick out a company just because it does well with the fundamental analysis. The company may be good, but if it has already reached its peak, it is unlikely that you can make money from this option. Of course, you could also miss out if you avoid a company that has been stagnant for a bit of time, but has good name recognition and will have some big news released soon that changes where the stocks go. Combining the two analysis together will help you to make the decisions that are needed to pick out good stocks for day trading.

The trick with working inside of day trading is to learn how to put both the technical analysis and the fundamental analysis together. When both of these tools work together, they can give you more confidence on the stocks that you pick and with some practice, you will be able to make a great income from day trading.

Gambling and Speculation

One area that some new traders get confused about when starting day trading is how it differs from speculation and gambling. For one, if you work on day trading the right way, you can actually make money. It is not about chance like gambling is, day trading is more about careful planning and research to pick out the best stocks that will earn you a profit.

One of the main differences that you can see between speculation and investing is the risks that are taken for the trade. With day trading, you get to choose the amount of risk that you would like to take and the amount you choose will directly correlate with the amount that you can make. Most beginners will start with a low-risk option to learn the game and then when they get more familiar with it, they can increase the risk. The more risks that you take on, the more your day trading can become like a gamble because the risk will become so high that you lose control.

In speculation, you will choose to trade on all of the high-risk options, sometimes they don't even spend time looking over charts or determining which process is the best one for them to go with. They will see that a stock has a high reward attached with it and will just choose to trade on that one. If you are correct, you will make a huge amount of profit, but since the risk is so high, you are more likely to loose out big when you speculate, which is why the high-risk options in day trading become like gambling.

Most day traders are not going to work in this way. They understand that they could make higher profits from some of the higher risk stocks, but they are also conscious of the fact that they could lose a lot of money as well. They are more comfortable with being in control of their investments so they will choose lower risk options that may yield a lower return but makes it more likely they will at least get something back from the trade.

No matter what strategy you pick for day trading, you must make sure that you are thinking like an investor, not a gambler. When you think about the stock market as a gambler, you are more likely to take risks that are not necessary, allow your emotions to get into the mix, and end up losing a lot of money in the process. But when you think about the stock market as an investment, you are more likely to think your decisions through and you will gather the information that is needed to actually make some money. The gamblers are the ones who give day trading a bad name because they do end up failing and losing a ton of money in the process. But when you act like an investor with day trading, you are sure to see your income grow.

Learning how to do the right kind of analysis, either the technical analysis or the fundamental analysis, you are going to learn how to understand the market and how it works, and you will be able to use this information in order to get the most out of all trades. As you learn how the market is going to work, you may make a few bad trades in the process (something that even professional investors see happen on occasion). But over time you will get pretty good at reading the market and you can make the right decisions, with the right amount of risk that you are comfortable with, in order

to find success with day trading.

CHAPTER 5: ADDITIONAL DAY TRADING

STRATEGIES

The technical analysis and the fundamental analysis are great places to start when it comes to working in day trading, but you also need to work on a good strategy to make sure you are picking the stocks that work the best for you. There are actually quite a few different strategies that will work in day trading, but it is important to understand how they work because all of them work a little bit differently. They can all be successful so you simply need to pick the one that works the best for you and then stick with it.

It is sometimes tempting to skip around from one strategy to another when you first start out because you are uncertain about how all of them work or you are uncertain about how each one will work. But you need to pick just one strategy, learn how to use it properly, and then stick with it so that you can see success. Here we are going to talk about some of the best day trading strategies that you can use and while they don't guarantee success every time when used properly, they can increase your chances of getting a good return on investment from your day trading endeavors.

News trading

One strategy that is pretty successful in day trading is called news trading. With this strategy, you are able to predict some big changes that will happen in the stock market, or for a particular stock, before others can catch on to the news. When this strategy is successful, you are able to purchase the stocks that you would like before the news is released, usually at a lower price. Then when the news breaks, you will be able to sell the stock at a higher price so you can make a good profit.

This strategy is going to require you to do quite a bit of research ahead of time. You need to be able to read the news and recognize some signs in different stocks to tell when a big change will occur to change the value. You will find that some of the news is going to help increase how much the stock is worth. You would want to purchase the stock before the news breaks so you can get it for a low price and then when the news comes out, you can sell the stock when the price goes up. On the other side of things, it is also possible to read the news and realize when a stock is about to go down in price. If you already own the stock, you would want to sell it quickly before you lose out or you would want to avoid purchasing this stock at all since the price is likely to go down.

Range trading

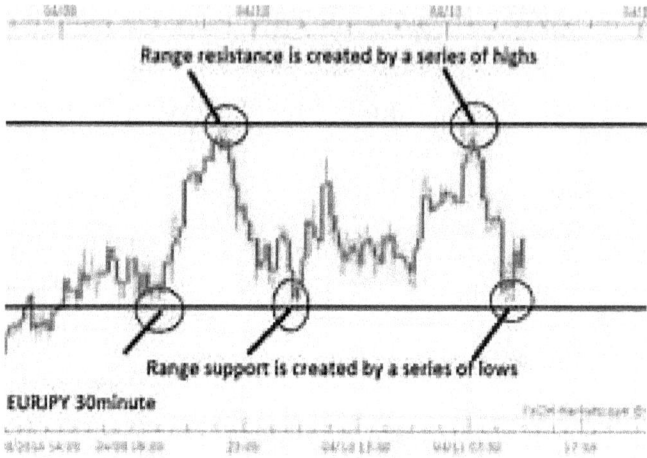

Range resistance is created by a series of highs

Range support is created by a series of lows

EUR/JPY 30minute

Another strategy that can help beginners make some money in day trading is known as range trading. With this strategy, you are able to identify the overbought and oversold areas for the stock. For this one, you need to be able to look at the support and the resistant areas. This is the one that you will want to work on if you notice that there are a few markets that end up meandering, or in markets that there seems to be a lot of up and down in the market, but you aren't able to find a trend or a pattern that goes with them.

Pairs trading

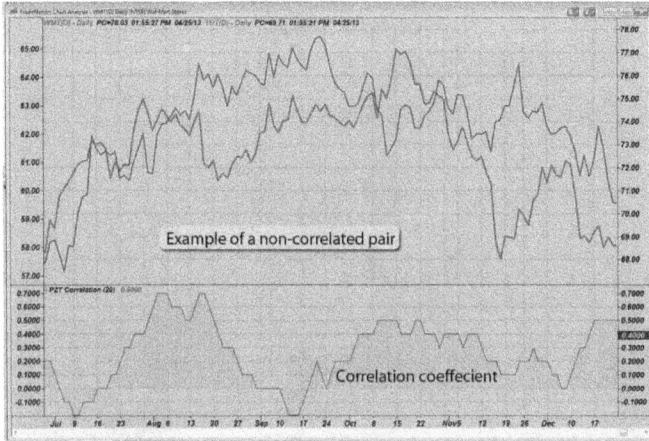

Example of a non-correlated pair

Correlation coeffecient

Many beginners like to work with the strategy that is called pairs trading. This strategy helps you to remain neutral in the market and it can match together a short position with a long position so you reduce your risks and can make some good money in the process. When you are a pairs trader, you are going to look for some weaknesses to occur in the market before going long on a stock that is underperforming and then going short on the stock that is over performing. This will effectively close up the position so when the gap closes back up, the market gets back to normal and you are able to make a profit from these positions.

You will find that the profit you are able to get from pairs strategy is going to come from the difference in price that will occur between your two instruments, or your two stocks, rather than from where they are both able to go inside the market. Basically what this means is that you will be able to get a profit if the long position goes up more than the short one, and you can make a profit can be made if the short position ends up going down more than the long one. This is why pairs trading can be so successful; it is possible to earn some money on different market conditions, even if there is an issue with low or high volatility or f the market starts to go in any direction.

The most difficult part of working on pairs trading is picking out the stocks that you want to invest in. There are actually quite a few options that you can work with, but you need to make sure that you are pairing the right ones together so you make a profit as well as picking the right one to go long on and the right one to go short on. If you are able to do this successfully, you can do a great job with pairs trading.

Contrarian trading

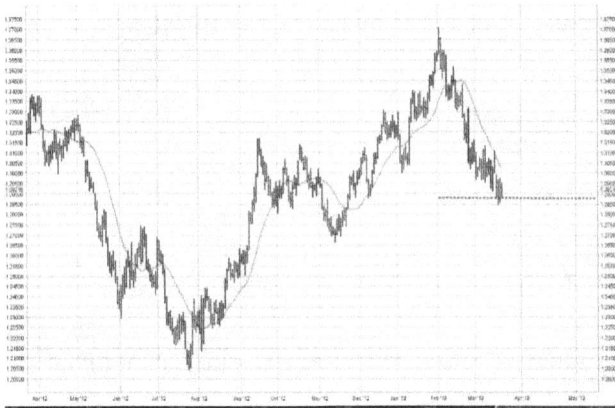

Contrarian trading is another option that you are able to use and it is going to be able to work against some of the other forms of trading that we have talked about so far. It goes against the other strategies because you are able to look at the market, and then go against it to find the assets that are performing poorly, but which you think will start to do well

67

soon. Sometimes there are some good stocks on the market, but for some reason or another, they are not performing the way that they should. With this strategy, you would find these stocks, purchase them at a low price, and then make a profit when their value goes up.

With the contrarian strategy, you are always looking for the motive for why people tell you certain things. You are going to believe that people are telling you the market is going up are simply doing this because they invested in the stock and they don't have the option to make some other purchases. When this starts to happen, the market is near or at the peak and making the purchase is going to cost you a lot of money. On the other side of things, if you hear that the market is in a downturn, it means that the other traders already sold their stocks and the market has already gone through a downturn. This is the perfect time to make a purchase because the stock market can only go up from here.

With the contrarian trading, you go with the idea that if you follow the same path that others do, you are basically passing up on some great opportunities and you will not be able to make the income that you desire. Others have already gotten to this stock and beat you to it, so jumping on means you will just lose out because the prices are already either too high for you to purchase or too low for you to sell. With this method, you are able to fight through some of this, and pick out stocks that go against the popular trend, in the hopes that you can jump on before others purchase them, and get a great sale in the process.

Momentum trading

It is also possible to work on a strategy that is known as momentum trading. When you are using this strategy, you are going to try and predict some of the trends that could occur in the stock market prices. If you are right, you will end up making a good profit in the process. There are a couple options that you can use to guess which way the momentum is going. First, you would take the time to watch the charts on a specific stock. By looking at these charts, you are able to find some of the patterns that are going on, a back and forth between the highs and lows and when you catch this pattern, it is easier to know when to purchase and when to sell.

Now, all stocks have some kind of trend that goes with it. Some will stay high for a bit, some will stay low for a bit, and others are always going up and down. But with momentum trading, you will be able to tell what direction a stock is going to head based on where it has been recently and in the past. For example, if you notice that a stock has a pretty steady trend of going up and down, you would be able to look at one of the downward trends and guess that the price is about to go up. This would be a good time to purchase so that you get that stock at a low price and can sell it at a higher one.

This can also be used in order to help you to know when to avoid a stock or when to sell a stock you already own. If you know the trend of a stock and notice that it has stayed high for a bit, it is time to sell the stock because the price is about to go back down. This would not be a good time to purchase the stock either because unless there is going to be some big news about the company, the price of the stock will not go up, and you will end up losing money in the process.

The momentum option is going to take a look at the history and the trends of the stock and figure out which way the stock is about to go. It is a pretty secure option to use because most stocks will follow the same trends over the long term unless something drastic happens with the market. It is often best to combine this one with the news strategy so you can tell if some big event is going to change how the stocks will behave and if they are going to leave their trends, even temporarily, so you can make adjustments to what you purchase and when you sell.

Heikin-Ashi trading

When you look at the charts for this one, you will notice that it looks like the candlestick chart, but the method of plotting and calculating the candles will be a bit different compared to using the candlestick chart. On a traditional candlestick chart, each of your candlesticks will show up for numbers including the low, high, close, and open prices. But with the Heikin-Ashi candle, we are going to be able to do our candles based on some information that came from the previous candle.

Some of the things that we would look for with the Heikin-Ashi candles include:

- The close price. The Heikin-Ashi candle is going to be the average of the open, close, high, and low price.

- Open price: for this candle, it is going to look at the previous candle and look at the average of the close and open.

- The high price: for these candles, the high price is going to be chosen from one of the high, close, and open price, based on which one has the highest value.

- Low price. The high price on this candle is going to be chosen from the close, open, and high price from the previous candle that will have the lowest value.

All of the candles in this method are going to be related to each other because the close and the open price on each candle is calculated with the information from the previous candle. You will look at the open and close price of the previous candle to determine the new candle that you create.

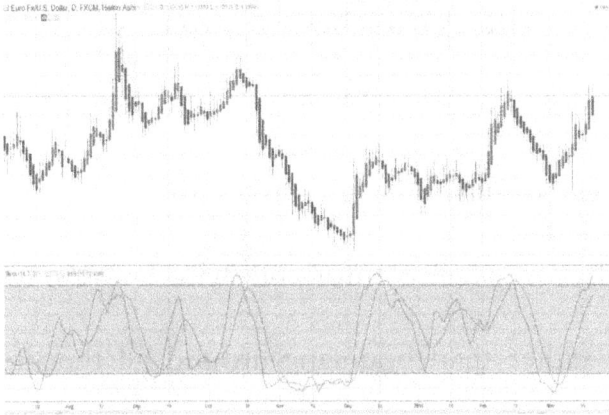

The chart above is an example of how the Heikin-Ashi candles would look. The red is going to show the bear markets, when it would be a good time to make a purchase of the stock to get it for the lowest price and the green would be the bullish markets, when it may be a good time to work on selling the stocks for a good profit.

Picking out the strategy that you are going to use when working in day trading can be really important. It is going to help you to understand how the market works, how to recognize certain signs inside of the market and to ensure that you are taking the risks that you feel the most comfortable with. All of these strategies can be successful and sometimes traders will pick a few of them to combine to get the best results. The important thing is to pick out a strategy that you feel comfortable with and then stick with that one, rather than bouncing around all the time. When you are able to do that, you will find that even as a beginner, you will be able to realize a profit.

CHAPTER 6: THE BEST PLATFORMS FOR DAY TRADERS

When starting with day trading, it is important to have the right tools. If you have the wrong broker or get started with the wrong platform, you are setting yourself up for failure from the beginning. Checking out a few different platforms will make it easier for you to start out right, helps you to avoid some of the fees that are common with some of the lower quality platforms, and can increase your money earning potential.

There are several things that you can consider when picking out a platform. The first thing to look at is the reputation of the platform, asking questions about how well they help other investors make money or if there happens to be a lot of complaints against poor customer service and high fees with this particular company. A smart investor also needs to look at the benefits that each platform brings, such as the fee structure, what types of trading they allow, and whether you get along with the broker or not before picking out the platform that you want to use.

Luckily, there are many great financial platforms you can choose to work with so you have options and can shop around to find some of the best platforms to increase your earnings.

Financial brokers in the United States

If you are working on day trading in the United States, there are many financial brokers you can choose. With that being said, there are some brokers who are able to stand above the rest of the advisors and firms based on their ease of use, knowledge about the market, and their performance. As a beginner, it may be a good idea to start with one of the following companies to help out with your day trading:

- TD Ameritrade

- Fidelity

- Charles Schwab

- E-Trade

- Merrill Edge

- Scottrade

- TradeKing

- OptionsHouse

- TradeStation

- Capital One Investing

Financial brokers in Europe

Depending on your strategy with day trading, you may find that you want to work with a financial platform based in Europe. This can also work well if you plan to expand out your portfolio and would like to work in a new market.

There are some great markets to work with in Europe as well including:

- Avatrade

- XM

- LMFX

- eToro

- NetoTrade

- Markets.com

- Oanda

Picking out a good financial platform for your day trading is critical when starting your investment. When you shop around and check with a few of these brokers in order to see what services they offer, what fees they charge, and even look into their reputation to make sure you pick the platforms that meet your day trading needs.

CONCLUSION

Thank for making it through to the end of *A Beginner's Guide to Day Trading: Discover How to Be a Day Trading King*. Let's hope it was informative and able to provide you with all of the tools you need to achieve your goals of

The next step is to find a good financial broker to help you to get into the day trading market. You will find that there are many strategies that you can use, but if you find the one that helps you to think about your decisions and do the research, you are sure to see some great return on investment in the long run.

Day trading is not about gambling, it is about knowing the market and learning how to make smart decisions on when to purchase and when to sell your stocks in order to make a profit. This guidebook took the time to show you the different strategies that are successful in day trading, even for beginners. This can be a really successful choice for making a

profit on your investment and this guidebook will be able to

help you get started!

DAY TRADING: THE ULTIMATE GUIDE TO DAY TRADING: UNCOVERING DAY TRADING PROFIT MAKING SECRETS

DESCRIPTION

While anyone can make a few trades per day, and maybe even find some success while doing so, if you are interested in day trading on a serious level then there are many distinctive characteristics and traits that you should strive to embody on a regular basis. Likewise, there are certain strategies you should know in order to give yourself a fighting chance. If you are interested in doing more than simply surviving in the world of day trading, if you are looking to truly thrive then *Day Trading: The Ultimate Guide to Day Trading* is the book that you have been waiting for.

Inside you will find everything you need to up your day trading game as quickly and effectively as possible. This includes characteristics that all good day traders should possess and how to implement them in your own life. You will also find important tips and tricks to maximize your overall trade effectiveness as well as frequently made mistakes and the easiest ways to ensure that you don't fall into their traps.

You will also find a complete breakdown of the tools that every competent day trader needs as well as specific suggestions to ensure that know what the professionals are using and where to find them. Finally, you will find five of the most effective strategies for gaining success while day trading with in-depth explanations to ensure you can put them into action ASAP. It doesn't matter what markets, timeframes or risk/reward ratios that you favor, *Day Trading:*

The Ultimate Guide to Day Trading has the right strategy for you.

Being a successful day trader is all about having the knowledge, not just to know where the market is going but how to best take advantage of where it's been. This is what separates the novices from the experts and those that boast a successful trade percentage from those who wouldn't be able to trade at a 50 percent success rate if their lives depended on it. So, what are you waiting for? Get ready to tap into that knowledge and buy this book today.

Inside you will find

- The importance of finding a way to motivate yourself without worrying about external stimuli

- Tips for successfully choosing the right trade at the right time a statistically relevant portion of the time

- The importance of timing and how to ensure you always choose the right time to enter or exit a trade

- The five most important attributes for every successful day trader to have and how to implement them in your own life

- The difference between the butterfly spread and the modified butterfly spread and when to use each for the best results

- What value areas are and how to put them to work effectively for you

- Why you shouldn't be trading options without considering hedging your trades

- How scalping Bollinger bands can take your forex trading game to the next level while only increasing your risk a small amount

- The best way to jump into futures trading while maintaining a reasonable level of risk

- *And more...*

INTRODUCTION

Congratulations on downloading *Day Trading: The Ultimate Guide to Day Trading* and thank you for doing so. For many traders, even those who are experienced working in various markets, taking the next step and day trading can be a daunting process. The speed at which day trading takes place, coupled with the much greater potential for loss, as well as gains, means that you would do well to learn as much as possible before diving in.

To that end, the following chapters will discuss everything you know to begin day trading on the right foot. First, you will learn about many of the characteristics that successful day traders embody. Next, you will learn tips for ensuring that your time spent day trading is as effective as possible as well as common mistakes that many day traders make so that you don't fall into these common traps yourself. You will then learn about many of the tools that are crucial to a day trader's success including specific options to consider based on what is currently popular with the day trading crowd.

With the generalities out of the way, you will then read in-depth accounts concerning five different day trading strategies including the modified butterfly spread, value areas and order flow sequencing, forex options hedging, scalping Bollinger bands and trading future spreads. Each of these strategies will go beyond the basics in an effort to provide you with all the details to put them into practice yourself in an effort to maximize your profits as effortlessly as possible.

There are plenty of books on this subject on the market, thanks again for choosing this one! Every effort was made to ensure it is full of as much useful information as possible, please enjoy!

CHAPTER 1: SUCCESSFUL DAY TRADER

CHARACTERISTICS

While making a few successful trades every day is relatively straightforward, if you hope to take your skills to the next level there are several things you can strive to do to maximize your success. No two day traders are exactly alike, but the most successful in the field tend to exhibit many of the same positive traits and characteristics outlined below.

Get a jump on the day: Just because the market doesn't open until 9:30 am, that doesn't mean this is when your day should begin. Successful traders spend the early morning hours checking in on the international markets so they know what the day is likely to bring. The Western economy doesn't exist in a vacuum, understanding the foreign markets makes it easier to predict upcoming changes at home. Remember, having an accurate macro view is a key part of utilizing micro changes effectively.

Become a master: In order to truly master a new skill, be it ballroom dancing or day trading, you need to be willing to put in the practice time. It takes 10,000 hours to become a true master which works out to eight hours a day for 42 months. While certain people are always going to get lucky, if you hope to see significant success you have to be willing to put in the work up front. Day trading is a marathon, not a sprint, slow and steady wins the race.

Never stop learning: The most successful day traders are not the ones who have mastered existing plans and strategies, they are the ones who understand that new alternatives are always taking shape. Getting in the habit of always remaining on the lookout for the next big thing is one of the best ways to separate yourself from the amateur day traders who will never be truly successful. The market is constantly in flux which means that any analysis you do is going to have a shelf life of less a week, at most. Resting on your laurels when it comes to what you know is a surefire way to curtail your profits. Remember, learning leads to earning.

Forge your own path: The best day traders don't just automatically go along with the crowd. They trust their intuition and their research, even if it means making trades that aren't on anyone else's radar. The biggest wins come from trades that are against the mainstream and knowing when to execute is what separates average traders from masters. The key here is to know the difference between trades that have been hyped up and those that have potential based on facts alone. Much daily market movement is caused by sheep who follow what the crowd is doing, be a wolf instead. If you don't feel as though your intuition is as strong as it could be, the solution is to keep studying and do more trading. Early success will improve your confidence and make it easier to trust in yourself no matter what.

Be ready for anything: The best traders are the ones that know they have a quality plan and also have the ability to stick to it without letting their emotions get in the way. There is more to being successful than blindly following your plan, however, you also need to be capable of understanding when things have changed enough to make it irrelevant. The easiest way to do this is to know the state of the market as it currently stands and where it is likely to go while the trading day is in progress. Whatever you do, it is important to keep a firm grip on your emotions as there is no quicker way to fail than to start thinking with your heart as opposed to your head.

Know yourself: In order to be a successful trader in the long term, it is crucial that you understand your strengths as well as your weaknesses. Doing so will enable you to capitalize on the one while shoring up the other. This is a key part of minimizing risk; which, in turn, is key to maximizing your profits. The easiest way to go about determining what your strengths and weaknesses are is to keep a trading journal. Keeping tabs on all the specifics related to each trade you make will allow you to look for patterns that otherwise might remain hidden. Once you are aware of any negative patterns you might fall into, you will be well on your way to mitigating them.

Know when to act: You can do all the research you like, if you don't have the ability to pull the trigger when the time is right then you will never be a successful day trader. The market is fickle, especially in the charts that day traders favor, which means that huge gains or losses can occur in moments. As such, you need to be able to make split second decisions and know that they are the right ones when money is on the line. This isn't the same as following your gut or getting lucky, it is the skill to read new situations and react in real time and to be able to do so effectively time and again.

Internal motivation: In order to be a successful day trader, you need to be able to motivate yourself to keep at it, even when the going gets tough. Making trading your job means that there will be no one looking over your shoulder telling you to get to work, that motivation will need to come from within. Only by looking within and finding the personal drive to succeed will you be able to do what needs to be done regardless of the cost. This is where the discipline to go from good to great comes from and it is not something that can be learned, you are either self-motivated or you aren't.

Have enough trading capital: In order to be a successful day trader you need to have the right amount of capital at your disposal. If every trade is life or death then this will skew your motivation and potentially keep you from making trades that will likely be successful. The most successful traders know their limits and never step outside them. No trader can be right one hundred percent of the time, and when the odds aren't in your favor you need to know that you can come back from the loss and try again. This is why it is recommended that you never put more than two percent of your total trading capital into a single trade. Sticking to this rule will keep your potential for loss at a reasonable level and help to ensure that you are able to manage your emotions at all times. Ensuring an emotional distance from all of your trades means that you will always be able to listen to reason, improving your overall trade percentage in the process.

Never be afraid to think things through: While making split-second trades is crucial to finding success as a day trader, that doesn't mean you should do so without thinking the state of things through first. It is important to always know exactly what your decisions are going to lead to, even if it means missing out of the maximum amount of potential profit to do so. While trading, your goal should always be to make decisions that are proactive, never reactive.

CHAPTER 2: TIPS TO MAKE DAY TRADING AS PROFITABLE AS POSSIBLE

While day trading successfully is always going to involve a little luck, that doesn't mean there is nothing you can do to improve your averages. Consider the following tips and tricks to help you end every day further in the black than when you started.

Choosing the right trades

A successful trade is always going to be built on a measured approach. To ensure this is the case you are going to want to begin by choosing the type of stocks that align with your goals as well as your temperament. Furthermore, you are going to want to take any external knowledge you might have into account when choosing the right stocks to focus on. As an example, if you were previously in the medical field then stocks based on pharmaceutical companies might be a good choice. Regardless, it is important to always take the following three main aspects of every trade into account before you make any decisions.

Timeframe: First and foremost, you are always going to want to trade in a timeframe that you are comfortable with. Doing otherwise will simply lead to scenarios where you are not at your best because you are impatient or just plain nervous. If you are still trying to improve your overall trade percentage you will likely want to stick to the 5-minute charts until you can be truly comfortable dealing with the potential for risk that holding stocks overnight can cause. You will also need to consider if you prefer micromanaging trades all day every day or prefer doing all your research over the weekend to pursue weekly trades come Monday morning. Micromanaging trades leads to short-term gains while weekly trades produce long-term gains.

Trading tactics: When it comes to choosing a methodology to use while trading, it is important to focus on what works for you instead of bouncing around based on what is popular in the moment. It is important to remember that every trader is going to have good days and bad days and if you can find a methodology that is successful at least 60 percent of the time then you are well on your way to success. Switching your tactics constantly is only going to skew your stats so you won't be able to determine the true cause of either your successes or your failures. What's worse, changing constantly will make it difficult for you to learn the intricacies of the methodologies you use, meaning they will be less effective in even more scenarios.

Tools of the trade: Much like methodologies, it is important to find a few trading instruments that work for you and focus on making the most of them. This is preferable to using a little bit of everything as you will be able to more closely tailor what you use to match your trading style. The best way to determine what is going to be useful to your style is by focusing on instruments that match the timeframes you frequent most often.

Attributes

There are several different attributes that all day traders should strive to embody. While not everyone will naturally be able to access them from the start, they can all be improved with practice.

Patience: After you have found a trade that you think is going to be fruitful, it is important to exhibit patience and find the perfect moment to pull the trigger. This is why it is useful to always determine your entry and exit points beforehand, so that there is less of a chance of emotion getting in the way.

Additionally, if the trade doesn't reach those numbers then you need to have the patience to wait for a better option to come along. If you decide to chase the potential for profit by altering your exit and entry points on the fly then all you are going to do is to skew the effectiveness of your plan. Once this occurs you lose regardless of the outcome as even if you profit from the sudden change you are reinforcing bad habits that will ultimately cause you harm in the long run.

Belief: Having belief in the trading plan or system that you have created is crucial when it comes to day trading because no plan is flawless. Day trading plans only prove successful when used reliably in the long term and swapping things around constantly is going to skew the percentages against you. Remember, a good plan or system gives you an edge, otherwise you are essentially just gambling and there are more effective ways to gamble than with the stock market.

Believe in yourself and your system and you will see greater profits overall.

Objectivity: It is important to never get too attached to a given stock and always approach every trade from a point of objectivity. Losing this objectivity can cause you to make mistakes like doubling down on a stock that has gone out of the money or staying in past the logical exit point. The same goes for listening to outside sources. Once you have committed to a given trade the only source you will want to listen to is your trading plan, everything else may as well be white noise. Each trade should be analyzed based on its relative merits, if you do so then you should trust yourself and let the rest take care of itself.

Expectations: Believing in yourself is an important part of day trading successfully but having measured expectations is crucial as well. Above all you need to have a realistic understanding of what your profits are likely to be before you start any new trade. Having realistic expectations in this way will help to prevent you from letting emotions get the better of you and lead to more reliable trades overall. Keeping your expectations in check means understanding the risk and reward of every trade. Remember, short term trades are more likely to lead to small, safe gains while long term trades are riskier and can end in greater gains.

Motivations: It is important to understand your own motivations in order to be true to yourself and your trading style. It is also important to understand the various motivations that different commodity markets have if you hope to trade in them successfully. In order to determine the current motivations of the commodities you favor, the first thing you will want to do is to consider the major players in the market in question. With that in mind, you can then watch the commodities themselves and determine how they are moving and why. Once you are familiar with what is currently happening you can then compare that to the historical movement. When taken as a whole you can then determine how the moves the major players make affect changing market conditions and predict future movement from there.

Putting thoughts into action

Keeping everything in mind at all times can be challenging, if you never put what you have learned into practice, however, then you will never grow as a trader. What's worse, you will never turn a reliable profit. Once you know what you are doing you will then want to keep track of your trades as soon as they begin and don't be afraid to bail on a trade when it suddenly goes south. Remember, a small loss now is always preferable to a bigger loss in the future. Additionally, it is important to keep in mind that there will not always be a worthwhile trade to be made. Just because you are a day trader doesn't mean you need to be trading every second of every day.

Learning the most intricate parts of the markets you favor isn't something that can be taught, it can only be learned with practice. What's more, sometimes mood is going to skew unexpectedly and through everything out the window for a time. Ultimately it all comes down to Warren Buffet's number one rule, "the only hard and fast rule is to never lose money." Stick to this rule and you can never go wrong.

CHAPTER 3: IMPORTANT DAY TRADING

MISTAKES TO AVOID

While it is impossible to become a master day trader without making, and learning from, mistakes. There are plenty of pitfalls that being aware of will allow you to avoid without stepping into them yourself. Remember, forewarned is forearmed.

Chasing tops and bottoms: Some strategies are effective when put into play near potential turning points. These are in the minority however and picking tops or bottoms is a risky proposition, at best. It is common for many traders to invest extra money into securities that seem either too low or too high, breaking the cardinal rule of a two percent trading limit in the process. This impulse should be avoided at all cost in favor of focusing on the major move that is inbound.

Starting to one side of range-bound markets will lead to better overall results practically all of the time.

Not getting while the getting is good: Many day traders have an adequate entry plan but then move forward without determining an exit plan that is just as effective. This, in turn, leads to scenarios where they either get out too early, too late or end up with an investment instead of a trade. If you find it difficult to know when to exit gracefully, you will want to focus on adding detailed technical specifications to your exit strategy. Once you put these specifics into place, it is important to monitor them and change them as needed as the market evolves.

Wasting time trying to get even: If you ever hope to be a master day trader then you need to factor failure into your long-term plan. Not only will this make it easier to prevent emotion from getting the better of you, it will help you make fewer mistakes down the line as well. Remember, it is important to focus exclusively on the numbers and not pin your self-esteem or personal image to individual trades. Focusing on the price action will allow you to block out thoughts about breaking even or magic numbers and improve your trade percentage as a result. Determining if a day was a success or a failure isn't something you can do until the market closes and it is useless, and destructive, to try.

Following relative trends: Existing trends in the market can be a potential signpost for future movement but they are far from guaranteed. It is completely natural for the market to fluctuate as much as 20 percent on either side of the average at any given time. As such, if you jump on an apparent trend without researching it thoroughly you can find yourself attached to a momentum play that will never materialize. Instead, it is important to consider each apparent trend through the lens of three distinct time frames for the best results. If you are fond of short-term trades then daily, hourly and weekly charts are recommended. If you prefer long-term trades then you will want to stick to weekly, daily, and monthly charts instead.

Unduly narrowing your focus: Every time you make a trade it is important to remember that it doesn't exist in a vacuum. Not taking this into account will cut into your trading capital with a steady stream of preventable losses. A better solution is to instead take a macro view on all of your current trades. This means keeping tabs on market leads and looking for capital that is likely to move in general derivatives. These derivatives are key as they highlight the underlying connections between markets that ensure they move in the same ways. Remember, the greater your scope the more effective you will be.

Letting strong opinions affect your trading: While everyone has opinions, effective day traders know that letting them influence your daily trades is a recipe for disaster. The only thing you need to rely on in order to trade effectively is math, anything else is just going to get in the way. Observe and analyze political and economic events, don't get caught up in them.

Having the wrong timing: Finding a potentially profitable trade is only half the battle, you also need to learn when to pull the trigger for the best results. Making the right move at the wrong time costs day traders collectively millions of dollars a day. This is not to say that you need to wait for everything to align perfectly before you make your move. Rather, you are going to want to get a feel for the moment that things are right enough and act accordingly.

To do so you are going to want to be aware of relative trend, understand the current strength of the weekly cycle and keep an eye on accumulation and distribution indicators. Above all else, never move on a hunch or tip without doing the required research as all you are likely to do is throw your commission fees away.

Averaging down: While averaging down is rarely the primary plan, it is easy to let it happen if you aren't actively planning against it. The resources spent holding a weak position can almost always be better spent elsewhere as every trade costs you time and weak positions are likely to cost you money as well. Keep in mind that every failed trade means that your next successful trade needs to pay out extra just to help you break even for the day and then even more to get ahead. If your starting trade capital isn't that great, averaging down can represent days, or even weeks, you are going to need to spend crawling back to square one. If you subsist on short-term trades then you need to be ready to exit as soon as forward momentum slows or, at worst, starts to slip backward.

Not accurately calculating risk and reward: Risk and reward are naturally a part of every trade. This doesn't mean they are always equal, however, and if you don't take the difference into account you can make the wrong moves without even realizing it. This is why it is important to set daily trading limits as it will help you to bring things into focus. If a given trade is risky enough to warrant possibly losing ten percent of your daily loss limit then you will want to ensure it will pay out at least twice, if not three times as much to balance out the risk. Regardless, making ten smaller trades that are more likely to be successful is almost always going to be a better choice.

CHAPTER 4: THE BEST TOOLS OF THE TRADE

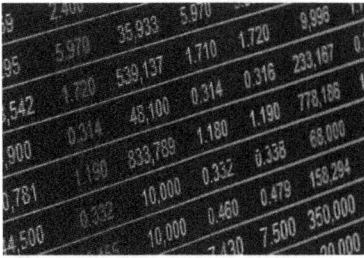

Perhaps more so than any other type of trading, the tools you employ while day trading are extremely important if you hope to turn a profit on a regular basis. Due to the tight timeframes that day traders operate under, every second counts which is why the tools, software and platforms outlined below bear serious consideration.

Tools

Current hardware: You don't necessarily need a top of the line laptop or computer in order to run a majority of the available trading software. You do, however, need to have something that exceeds the minimum required specifications if you want to avoid crashes or lag at the worst possible moments.

Primarily, this means you are going to want to have plenty of available ram to allow you to multitask as needed. As you develop a need for more advanced software, your hardware needs are going to increase as well. While these costs can really add up when new hardware is purchased all at once, this is rarely necessary. Instead you can purchase parts piecemeal overtime and grow your hardware's capabilities as your skill as a day trader improves.

Once you really get serious, you are going to want to run at least two monitors at once in order to trade on one and do research and track results on the other. This, in turn, means that you will need a higher quality dedicated video card with space for multiple inputs as an integrated option just won't cut it. At this point, depending on your system, you may need to look into liquid cooling options in order to ensure your system doesn't overheat in the middle of a major trade.

Additionally, you are going to want to invest in the highest available internet speed that you can find. Currently 1 gigabyte speeds are available in major markets, while something around 100 mbps is plenty fast for most systems. While having access to that speed is all well and good, it is important that you have a modem and router that can keep up as they will be the major bottleneck in this scenario. While you are in contact with your internet service provider, you are likely going to want to consider reinstalling a landline as well, just in case you find yourself unable to complete a trade in any other way. Having a hardline to your brokerage can be the difference between success and failure of a major trade, more than worth the $10 a month a phone line costs these days.

Brokerage: Many traders choose their first online brokerage when they are first getting started in trading and never think about their choice again. This is a big mistake, however, because an advanced trader's needs are very different from those of a beginner. As such, once you have some trading experience under your belt it is important to reevaluate your previous choice to determine if you truly made a good decision. First things first, in order to see what your available options are, you are going to want to visit the forums of your favorite day trading website and see what other traders have to say.

Once you have a suitable list, the next thing that you are going to want to consider is the fees that each offers, as well as any fringe benefits they provide. If you already have a trading platform and other online tools that you have a strong preference for, take special care to consider other brokerages who support them or you risk having to learn the ins and outs of new software from scratch. It is also important to choose an online brokerage from your home country or, barring that, one that operates somewhere that provides proper oversight for such things. While some foreign brokerages might have cheaper fees, putting your money in the hands of a company without the right oversight puts you at risk of losing your trading capital every single day.

Last but not least, you are going to want to see what type of customer service the brokerages that stand out to you provide. When it comes to customer service, you aren't going to want to listen to reviews, it is best to see for yourself. To do so, you are going to want to call the brokerage in question and see how long it takes you to get in touch with a real person. While this won't often be a necessity, if you have to call your brokerage it is likely an emergency and you will want to know that someone is waiting on the other end of the line.

As a new potential customer, you may need to expect a call back from the brokerage. If they don't get back to you with 24 hours, move on. If the brokerage treats new potential customers with such disdain, consider how they are likely to respond once they already have your money. Assuming their live support is up to par, you should then try emailing the brokerage with a few questions and see how quickly they respond as this will likely be your primary mode of contact in the future. While this can be time consuming, customer service is what separates the best brokerages from the pack and its importance cannot be over emphasized.

Day trading tools online: There is no shortage of available online tools when it comes to helping you maximize your day trading efficiency. The first thing you will want to find is a financial calendar that meets your needs. Ideally, this will provide a collection of importance events, a variety of customizable dates and also details on several different markets. If you dabble in the forex market you will also want a currency convertor that shows the changes to various currencies in real time as well as convertor that displays the range a pair of currency have inhabited over a definable period of time.

You should also find a calculator that will help determine pivot points as well as relevant Fibonacci numbers. These tools allow you to keep up to date on meaningful trends, keeping you in the know when it comes to important details that are easy to miss otherwise. Similarly, you also want to find a heat map that you trust to show you trades that are currently popular and a volatility monitor so you can keep tabs on the mood of the market.

Platforms to consider

These days there are so many different trading platforms that finding the right one can be needlessly complex. The list below helps to simplify things somewhat by gathering together those that are most popular at the moment. This doesn't mean you shouldn't do your own research if there is something specific you are looking for it is only to help point you in the right direction.

OptionsHouse.com: This is a low frills trading platform that is perfect for those who just want to focus on trading. It offers a suite of modifiable tools, no minimum account balance and a flat commission rate of $4.95 for each trade.

InteractiveBrokers.com: At the other end of the spectrum, this site requires $10,000 up front, though the requirements aren't as steep if you are under the age of 25. They take $.005

from each traded share and also offer a vast option base include forex, precious metals, futures and more.

Ameritrade.com: Frequently referred to as the best trading platform on the market today, this site charges a flat fee of $9.99 per trade. They off a low required balance, multiple internal trading platforms and access to curated research. Alternately, they also offer a secondary platform called Trade Architect which is ideal for those who are looking for a simple and straightforward platform.

TradeStation.com: This site boasts of its fast order execution and charges a varying commission on trades that is somewhere between $5 and $10 based on the volume of the trade. They also require a $5,000 minimum account balance and a $99 monthly fee though this is waved with a large enough monthly trade volume. Their trade platform is also renowned for being quite robust.

Trade software

Day trading software is evolving practically at the speed the market changes. As such, if you hope to maintain the greatest advantage possible it is important to update the software you use on a regular basis. The options below are some of the most commonly used software on the market today.

eSignal: This software includes a highly rated mobile application along with charting and analyzing capabilities said to be the best in its class. Additionally, it provides multiple alternatives for charting and scanning both individual and groups of stocks. They also provide a wealth of customizable chart options when it comes to indicators including momentum MACD, distribution, volume, accumulation and more. If you are looking to continue your day trading education they also offer trading education seminars, newsletters and forums.

Multichart: If you are looking for a way to view as many up to the minute data streams as possible, this is the software for you. Once you find the streams you are looking for it also allows you to create charts with data from numerous sources. The options for charting are vast as well; including, drawing, 3D charting, back testing and several strategy and management options. What's more, it allows you to choose a pricing plan based on the tools you plan to use.

NinjaTrader: This easy to use and affordable software is a great place to start if you are just starting to use more advanced day trading software. It features a simple and intuitive charting function that doesn't sacrifice anything when it comes to power or stat tracking. It provides users the ability to track executions and account positions and even trade automatically. It also allows users to scan the market in real time according to predetermined criteria.

Trade-Ideas: Knowing how to pick the few stocks that are going to move in a given day is a crucial part of day trading successfully. The best way to do so is via a stock scanning software and the best stock scanning software on the market is from Trade-Ideas. It includes loads of predefined searches including biggest gainers/losers, turbo breaks, volume spikes, HOD movers plus hundreds of different custom filters to ensure you can easily find what it is you are looking for whatever it may be.

CHAPTER 5: TRADING STRATEGY: MODIFIED
BUTTERFLY SPREAD

 When trading options, many day traders content themselves with utilizing calls and puts to make a profit from market decision or maybe using covered calls to generate income. There are more promising alternatives out there, however, one of which is the butterfly spread. The butterfly spread allows knowledgeable traders to pinpoint trades that are likely to generate a greater amount of profit for a limited amount of risk. The modified butterfly spread, discussed below, takes things a step further.

Modified spread compared to traditional spread

Standard butterfly: To understand what sets the modified butterfly spread apart, a look at the standard butterfly may be helpful. To perform the basic butterfly spread you utilize three calls or puts in a 1/2/1 configuration. The first call is purchased at a strike price comparable to the price of the underlying asset, another pair is purchased at a great price and a third is purchased at a price that is greater still. If dealing in puts, the strike prices descend in order instead.

The end result is a neutral trade that will generate a profit as long as the underlying asset stays within the range of the three strike prices. It is also useful when it comes to making directional trades by setting all of the strike prices above or below the current price. When utilized properly, this strategy ensures a low and well-defined level of risk with a reliable potential for profit and a relatively high chance of generating a significant rate of return.

Modified butterfly spread: The advanced form of this strategy has similar goals but differs from the simple version in a few key ways. Most importantly, it provides the user the opportunity to ensure that put trades are bullish and call trades are bearish. This occurs through the use of a 1/3/2 ratio which leaves just one price point where breaking even occurs. This, in turn, provides a sort of cushion that will allow you more leeway than the simple alternative.

As an example, assume an underlying asset is currently going for $194 a share. To execute the modified butterfly, you would then purchase a put at $194.50, sell three more at $190 and then buy a final pair at $175. The key takeaway here is the puts that are selling at 5 points below the at-the-money point and the second pair that are 20 points below.

While the current price is $194 this means you can break even if the price dips down to roughly $184 which means the strategy generated roughly 5 percent of downside protection points.

This, in turn, mean that the underlying asset would need to drop more than 5 percent before a loss would occur. The total amount of available risk in this scenario is roughly $2,000 which equates with the amount required to facilitate the trade. This loss amount would not come into play until the underlying asset dropped below $175. On the other hand, the amount of possible profit in this example would be roughly $1,000 which equates to approximately a 50 percent return on the initial investment assuming the underlying asset increases to $200. The strategy would also result in a $500 profit as long as the underlying asset doesn't move past $195.

While the modified butterfly spread is riskier than the traditional version, it also has a greater profit to risk ratio. The most common timeframe given for a modified butterfly spread is six weeks. It is an ideal strategy to use if you believe the underlying asset is going to remain mostly stable over the timeframe you have chosen. It is the perfect choice if you are hoping for capital gains on an underlying asset that is likely to remain in the middle of the road.

Important criteria

When determining the type of butterfly spread to use, it is important to be aware of the amount of capital you are willing to risk. You will also want to know the estimated return that risk will generate and the likelihood of success and failure. There is no right answer to these criteria, you will need to set your own limits in order to determine which type of butterfly spread is right for you.

The potential rate of return, along with the likelihood of it being generated are going to directly determine the amount of risk it is in your interest to move forward on. Performing your own risk/reward analysis is crucial in this instance and it is important to not rush into modified butterfly spread just for the purpose of mixing things up. Regardless, it is recommended that you only attempt the modified version if you have a sizeable amount of trade capital backing you up.

Options trading are ideal for day traders who are interested in maximizing their potential for flexibility which can help nullify a risk/reward ratio that is not as strong as you might like. As long as you use it sparingly, and in the right conditions, the modified butterfly spread is a useful way of maximizing this flexibility even more.

CHAPTER 6: TRADING STRATEGY: VALUE AREAS AND ORDER FLOW SEQUENCING

Order flow sequencing is a useful strategy that was developed by a trader who spent time at both Bear Stearns and Sungard Capital Markets before striking out on his own. The goal here is to document and track relevant prices as they apply to the movements of the major players in a given market to determine what they are likely to do next and when they are likely to start. This then, allows traders in the know to more easily identify points of greater liquidity along with greater risks with a level of transparency which can be applied to the market as a whole.

Order flow sequencing first gained popularity during the early years of the last century when market generated information first started to be a requirement for successful daily trading. When compared to other indicator based analysis methods, it works much more quickly while also focusing on the present instead of the past. This, in turn, means that when used properly you still have time to put the results into action.

When it comes to considering the major players in your market of choice, you may find it helpful to think of them in the way you would the House when it comes to casino gambling. Eventually the House will always win when given a long enough time frame. Major players have the same advantage and you will almost always find it harder to make money when trading against them instead of with them. Instead, it is much easier to travel in their wake and pick up the scraps from their big money trades. Depending on the market in question, major players include financial institutions, traditional banks, hedge funds, commercial traders, and even governments. You know you are on the right track if the entity you are following can make waves in your chosen market just by executing a single trade.

Understanding the trends that these entities generate will make it much easier for you to recognize and track potential advantageous movements based on order flow techniques. This results in a clear indication of the disruption that the major players leave in their wake. Tracking these disruptions will then make it much easier for you to be on the winning side the next time it happens.

Additionally, using order flow sequencing you will find that it is much easier to understand the how's and whys of price fluctuation in your chosen market.

Value areas

In order to use order flow sequencing effectively, the first thing you need to understand is the concept of value areas. Determining the value area is the best way to determine when any relevant major players are likely to make a move and what that move will be. Value areas can be broken down into three key parts, the high point, the low point, and the control point. High point value area levels are points where the volume and demand of a specific trade has left prices at an extremely expensive point. On the contrary, low point value areas are points where the price has dropped to a point that the major players are likely to come sniffing around. The control point value area is the point the price of the underlying asset is at when you do your analysis.

The easiest way to track the various value areas is through the use of a volume profile tool. This tool will let you compare historical volume levels to current levels over a predetermined period of time. All you need to do is then look for points of overlap between the past and the present. Comparing the control point to the previous high and low points will give you an idea of when the major players are likely to make a move. Ideally, you will want to find a control point that is near the historical low point. Points of confluence then indicate areas you should be interested in, though you won't want to consider them as they emerge. Utilizing this strategy on the fly is asking for trouble, it should primarily be used to plan ahead.

In this instance, volume is going to always be the simplest way to determine where the market is likely heading. If the volume is low then you can bet a shift is on the horizon. Remember, previous points of price rejection are the best places to start when determining where the next instance is going to occur. Keeping an eye on volume will also provide secondary confirmation as to when the major players are likely going to begin making purchases. Luckily, determining these guidelines is relatively straightforward, and depending on the results, can remain relevant for several weeks or longer with only minor tweaking.

Tracking sequences of order flow

After you are clear on the current relevant value areas, you will want to start tracking the general flow of orders as they come in. This will let you start to see the volume as it is created, giving you a window to prepare the proper entry and exit points. To put it another way, rather than looking at candlestick charts after the fact you can then watch the candlestick form. After you have established your value areas correctly is when being aware of order flow will truly start paying off.

At the start of each new day you are going to want to double check that any relevant value areas are still currently where you expect them to be. With that out of the way, it is a simple matter to find points where the volume will begin to dip while also pinpoint scenarios where price rejection will set in. Essentially, all you will need to do is discover the points where the high point and low point align with the volume levels you have already defined. This will give you likely entry and exit points.

While taking the time to determine all the details every single day might sound like a waste of time, it is important to consider the alternative. Specifically, all of your trades will end up being at the mercy of the major players in your chosen market. What's even worse, you won't know when you are working with incomplete information. If you find yourself making trades that are logical and follow your plan, but you still aren't seeing the results you like, then order flow sequencing may well be the missing piece of the puzzle.

Order flow tracking programs

There are several different order flow tracking programs available online these days. The following list of companies produce those that are currently the most popular, most effective and rated the highest in customer satisfaction

JIGSAW TRADING

Jigsawtrading.com: Jigsaw tools allow for the tracking of the stock, futures and forex markets as part of a standard suite of commonly used functions. They can track time and DOM sales along with several advanced features displayed in an intuitive fashion. Even better, their products are available for free for a limited time.

Ninjacators.com: The tools available at Ninjacators.com provide a greater access to customer settings while also allowing users to access every market for options in the world across every timetable you might expect. They are known for their unique split order flow tool which allows users to plot orders on both sides of a candle at once.

CHAPTER 7: TRADING STRATEGY: FOREX

OPTIONS HEDGING

The forex market has a reputation of being one of the more difficult markets to regularly make a profit from. However, this is only because of short scammers and traders who expect to see large returns in a short period of time due to the way the market often worked at the turn of the century. In order to ensure that the risk reward ratio balances out, it is important to have a proper way to hedge your trades. When utilized correctly, forex hedging provides traders with the opportunity to protect themselves regardless if they are planning to go long or short on a specific currency pair.

There are two primary ways of hedging a forex trade. The first is through using what are known as spot contracts which can be ineffective as they are often considered a short-term solution. The more effective of the two is known as a forex option. As the name implies, these trades provide the buyer the option, not the obligation, to buy or sell a currency pair at a set price at some point in the future. This strategy can be combined with several other strategies including bull and bear spreads, long straddles and long strangles.

Determine the risk

There are three steps to determine if a forex hedging strategy is the right choice based around the amount of risk you care to expose yourself to. The forex market is inherently riskier than most other markets which is what makes this strategy so crucial to long term success.

Risk analysis: The first thing that you need to do in order to hedge a forex trade properly is determine the level of risk that is inherent in the given currency pair. To accurately determine this, you will need to consider the implications of both letting the trade proceed normally and hedging it. This risk depends on the market and will likely be either visibly low or visibly high, if it is in the middle then you should hold off until a clear direction can be determined.

Consider your acceptable level of risk: Once you know the likely level of risk for the trade in question, the next thing you will need to do is determine if the level of risk is worth the extra costs that will be incurred by hedging it. This is as easy as looking at the potential gains and comparing them to the added costs and should be fairly straightforward.

Decide how to move forward: With the facts in front of you, the next step is to choose the strategy that is the most logical in the moment, remember, numbers don't lie. Your focus should be on the bottom line and the strategy that will generate the greatest return for your investment.

Forex hedging strategies

A good rule of thumb is the longer the term of any put options you use, and the lower the strike price, the more reliable the hedging strategy is going to be. While the initial cost is going to be significantly higher than not using a hedging strategy, the longer it stays in place the more cost effective it becomes. This makes it a particularly effective go-to when you are considering long term strategies. It is also much more cost effective to hedge indices as opposed to individual currency pairs.

You will also want to be aware that hedging will mitigate risk related to a dramatic change in value, but is ineffective when it comes to countering the risk that comes from general underperformance, something that will only be clear in the long term. This means it is really only worthwhile for risky trades that promise large payoffs. Additionally, you will need to keep in mind that not all forex brokers allow hedging so it is worth looking into before you mentally commit to anything.

Time extensions and put rolling: An excellent way to maximize the value of a hedge is to make a point of always choosing the put option with the greatest amount of available lead time. This is simply a matter of cost/benefit analysis as one option that lasts for six months is going to be much less expensive than two three month options. The ultimate marginal cost of maximizing your option provides you with the least expensive form of daily trade protection possible.

This is useful as you can turn a six-month option into a twelve-month option while still keeping the same strike price. This is known as rolling and it will let you take advantage of market changes as they appear. Assuming you have a strike price that is below the average market value you can keep an option rolling for years with only a minimal extra cost. This is exceptionally useful if you combine it with a highly leveraged investment that promises a large return as it mitigates a large amount of the potential risk.

Calendar spread: A calendar spread is created when both a long and short-term put option are bought and sold using the same strike price. The goal with this strategy is to let the shorter of the two puts expire at the end of its timeframe while letting the longer put serve as a hedge for future movement. When properly implemented, a calendar spread can generate a surprisingly cheap and effective hedge that can then be maintained indefinitely. It is important to consider the market prospects in the extreme long term before committing to this strategy as it can easily open you up to a significantly increased amount of total risk especially when it comes to underperformance.

CHAPTER 8: TRADING STRATEGY: SCALPING BOLLINGER STRATEGY

Forex scalping is commonly used in conjunction with short-term options in order to guarantee a profit. It works by opening and closing positions quickly in order to maximize the number of short, somewhat profitable, trades per day. When used properly you will hold on to individual positions for as little as a minute at a time. Many traders enjoy the Bollinger band scalping system because it is easy to accumulate profits in a short period of time in a fairly straightforward way. On the flipside, however, the sheer number of trades opens you up to increased risk when compared with the potential reward.

With that in mind, expert Bollinger band traders tend to accumulate gains faster than practically any other type of trader. If you already understand the basics of scalping and are looking for a way to maximize your profits in the forex market then choosing this strategy may be a no-brainer.

Bollinger band strategy 1

Strategy basics: This system revolves around an Exponential Moving Average along with a pair of Bollinger bands and is useful with virtually all currency pairs and time frames. With that being said, the most common and effective timeframe tends to be 5 minutes. Bollinger bands are a type of technical indicator which default to twenty periods with a standard deviation of two. However, with this strategy you want to set one band to twenty-one periods with a standard deviation of two and the other to twenty-one periods and a standard deviation of three.

The end goal here is to locate periods when the price touches a point that is between the pair of standard deviations. Once this occurs you will want to use a moving average of 200 as the guideline that allows you to accurately monitor the trend. If the price rises above the 200 point, then you can profit from long positions and if it drops then you can profit from short positions. At the same time, you will want to keep an eye out for a candle to form and close inside the space between the two deviations. If the opposite occurs then it indicates a reversal.

Parsing the data: When the conditions outlined above are met, then you know that you can open a trade at the start of the next candle with minimal risk. You will want to place a stop-loss either above or below the candles depending on the type of trade you are making. You may also want to set the target at the average of the pair of Bollinger bands with a second target set at either the upper or lower line, depending on the type of trade you are considering. This system has proven effective in virtually all situations as long as you take into account the price as it relates to the moving average of 200. This is a somewhat complicated strategy to put into practice, so making a few low-impact trades with it is recommended before moving to the big time.

Bollinger band strategy 2

This strategy is only effective with the GBP/USD and EUR/USD currency pairs in the 5-minute range. It is most effective when used in a market that is currently range bound with Bollinger bands that appear nearly flat. To use this strategy properly you will want to set the period of the bands to twenty with a standard deviation of two. It can work as expected during both the European and US trading sessions.

In order to use this strategy effectively you will want to buy when the bands are practically flat and the current price touches the lower of the two. You will then want to set a stop-loss that is 10 pips below the initial starting price. You will want to close out the trade once the price reaches the higher of the bands. If you are selling then you will want to do so when the price touches the top band and set a stop-loss that is 10 pips above the starting price. You will then close out the trade when the price reaches the lower of the two bands. This strategy can be more complicated than it first appears and practicing before putting into action is recommended.

One hour strategy

While not quite as short as the others, the goal of this strategy is to always make 50 pips with each trade. This system is proven effective in any trading session and works with pairs GBP/USD, EUR/USD, USD/JPY, NZD/USD, AUD/USD and USD/CAD. It will be most effective in a market environment that is range bound and features a pair of Bollinger bands that are virtually flat.

When buying and selling, if the current trend appears bullish, or the price touches the top band, you will want to generate an order with a stop-loss that is 35 pips below the starting price or at the previous low point, whichever is higher. Additionally, you will want to sell if the price rises 50 pips. You will also want to sell if the trend turns bearish or the price touches the lower of the bands. If you want to generate a sell order then you will use the same details as if the trend was bullish. As with the other strategies, practicing first is recommended as it is more complicated than it may first appear.

Extreme scalping

This system requires Bollinger bands that are set to twenty-one periods with a standard deviation of two. It is useful for timetables of one minute that have an RSI of fourteen, seventy, thirty. The goal here is to wait for the price to rise above one of the Bollinger bands while at the same time have the RSI increase to above seventy or to below thirty. The ideal target in this case is the dead center of the pair of bands with a pair of stop-loss five to seven pips higher and lower. As with the other strategies, practicing is recommended as it is more complicated than it may first appear.

CHAPTER 9: TRADING STRATEGY: FUTURES

SPREAD TRADING

While it requires a firm grasp of the complexities of the futures market, futures spread trading offers great rewards for those brave enough to utilize it. As such, it is often seen as the realm of the true professional and something every day trader should one day aspire to.

Common spread types: commodity futures

Inter-commodity futures: These futures involve contracts that are spread across various markets. As an example, if you believe that the wheat market is going to experience a high demand when compared to the corn market then you would buy wheat and sell corn. The specific prices for each don't matter as long as wheat prices beat corn prices.

Calendar Intra-Commodity: This spread looks at a single commodity between differing months of the year. As an example, if you believe that the wheat market is going to be stronger in November as opposed to June then you would go long in November and short in June. The specifics of the price don't matter as long as prices are higher in November than they are in June.

Bull futures: This spread looks at a single commodity under the assumption that the sooner month will boast a higher price than the later month. As an example, if you buy a bullish wheat future in May then you will want the price to be higher then, than when you sell it in June. For this type of future, it is important to keep in mind that near future contracts tend to move faster the further you get from the front month which gives this future its name. A bullish trader would then be one who buys in the front month in hope that it ends up moving at a greater rate than the deferred month.

Bear futures: This spread occurs if you purchase the same commodity in such a way that you are short in the front month and long on the deferred month. As an example, if you purchase wheat in May and sell it in June then you are hoping the prices are lower in May than they will be in June. For this type of future, it is important to keep in mind that near future contracts tend to move faster the further you get from the front month which gives this future its name. If you are confident that prices are at a low point then this is the type of spread you should consider buying into.

Futures spreads trading margins

It is important to keep in mind that if they are part of a spread then the individual margins on specific contracts are going to be reduced. As an example, if the margin on a specific wheat contract alone is $2,000, but if you go both long and short on wheat in the same year then the margin between the pair could be as little as $200. If you go both long and short on the same commodity in different years the margin will be roughly double, so in this case it would be about $400. The price differential occurs because the volatility of the spread is lower than that of the individual contract.

Essentially, the futures spread provides you with the ability to consider the market in slow motion. As such, if something serious happened in the wheat market then both contracts would be affected in the same way which provides a level of protection against the increased risk that the single contract doesn't have.

Futures spread pricing

The price of a futures spread can be determined by the perceived difference in the two contracts. To determine what the spread's pricing is going to be, all you need to do is subtract the deferred month price from the front month price. If the front month price is lower, the spread will be negative while if it is higher the spread will be positive. The tick values for both spreads and individual contracts are going to remain the same. As an example, if the price of wheat in June was $500 per bushel and in July it is $510 then the spread price is -$10. Meanwhile if the difference was $500 and $490 then the spread would be $10.

Types of markets

Contango markets: A market is considered Contango if the front month is obviously going to have a lower cost than the deferred month. Typically, this means the deferred month is going to cost slightly more than the front month due to cost to carry. The cost to carry takes into account the interest rate on the capital that is related to operating and owning the store that actually sells the commodity along with storage costs for keeping the commodity for the extra time along with additional insurance costs. This is considered the default type of market.

Backwardation markets: A market is thought to be in backwardation if the near months are valued highly when compared to the deferred months. Also known as an inverted market, it is the opposite of the standard market condition. It most commonly occurs if the market is in the midst of a bull phase which is often caused by an issue with the supply chain or a dramatic increase in demand coupled with a limited supply. The price differential occurs because the front months are going to feel the full brunt of the situation while it is more likely to be mitigated by the time the deferred months arrive. This is even more likely to be the case if the deferred month is in a different crop year from the front month.

Regardless of the current state of the market it is important to take seasonal concerns into account as well. Generally, gasoline prices are always going to be higher in the summer and the prices of heating oil, natural gas, and coffee are always going to be higher in the winter. Additionally, it is important to keep in mind that while all markets experience bullish and bearish periods, those experienced by the commodities are less consistent.

CONCLUSION

Thank you for making it through to the end of *Day Trading: The Ultimate Guide to Day Trading*, let's hope it was informative and able to provide you with all of the tools you need to achieve your financial goals, whatever it is that they may be. Just because you've finished this book doesn't mean there is nothing left to learn on the topic, expanding your horizons is the only way to find the mastery you seek.

The next step is to stop reading already and start preparing yourself to ensure that you are ready to do everything in your power in order to ensure that the time you spend trading is as profitable as it can possibly be. Armed with the tips, tricks, and strategies in the preceding chapters you will soon find that you can maximize your dedication and hard work to successfully conquer even the highest risk trades and claim the largest rewards.

That is not to say that major windfalls are going to come along every day, however. Just because you are ready to handle what day trading throws at you doesn't mean that you won't experience losses, and a great deal of them besides. Whatever you do, always keep in mind that crafting a trading plan that is sixty-five percent successful is considered extremely impressive. Only by keeping your expectations in check can you be sure that your emotions don't get the better of you and that you can survive day trading in the long term.

No matter how the minute to minute excitement makes you feel, it is always going to be more important to do your homework and faithfully execute on your plan no matter what, only then will you find the profits you seek. Don't forget, day trading is a marathon, not a sprint, slow and steady wins the race.

DAY TRADING: STRATEGIES ON HOW TO EXCEL AT DAY TRADING

DESCRIPTION

Day trading is an incredibly competitive field, but there is undoubtedly money to be made there if you know what you are doing. Unfortunately, even if you are familiar with what works in the stock market, you may not be prepared for the unique life of the day trader which is why it is helpful to have as many proven strategies up your sleeve as possible. If you have already dipped your toe into the waters of day trading and are looking to take your skills to the next level then *Day Trading: Strategies on How to Excel at Day Trading* is the book you have been waiting for.

Inside you will find a detailed breakdown of many of the most common patterns that are the secret to success for a wide range of day trading strategies whether you want to focus on the 1-minute chart, the 5-minute chart or even the 4-hour or daily charts. While many day traders focus on making as many trades as possible, the truth is that quality is just as important as quality, if not more, so and *Day Trading: Strategies on How to Excel at Day Trading* can show you how to only find the best trades while blocking out the rest of the market's noise.

While day trading is often placed on a pedestal by those who haven't yet mastered its ins and outs, the truth of the matter is that it is just like any other type of trading at its heart. If you can learn the strategies, and you have the mental fortitude to act only when your indicators tell you it's time and always get while the getting is good, then you can be a successful day trader. All you need is the strategies in this book to help you on your way.

So, what are you waiting for? Get ready to take control of your financial future and live the life you've always wanted! Get started now and buy this book today!

Inside you will find

- 14 different patterns that will help you determine the current momentum of the market no matter what the specifics.

- The 6 different types of gaps and how to make the most out of each of them before the fills set in.

- 8 different patterns and strategies for trading reversals to ensure you are always prepared to make the most from market movement.

- Everything you ever wanted to know about rising and falling wedges as well as the mysterious sideways wedge.

- *And more...*

INTRODUCTION

Congratulations on downloading *Day Trading: Strategies on How to Excel at Day Trading* and thank you for doing so. Day trading is an incredibly competitive field, but there is undoubtedly money to be made there if you know what you are doing. Unfortunately, even if you are familiar with what works in the stock market, you may not be prepared for the unique life of the day trader which is why it is helpful to have as many proven strategies up your sleeve as possible.

As such, the following chapters will discuss many of the most widely used day trading strategies to ensure you are on a level playing field when you head out to meet the competition. First you will learn about the benefits of momentum trading including the anatomy of momentum stocks, the right entry points and the right screeners to use to find them as well as the filters to use to make them worth your time. You will also learn several relevant chart patterns

170

and multiple different strategies to take advantage of them as completely as possible.

Next you will learn all about strategies for trading the gap including all the different types of gaps, what it takes to fill them and strategies to profit from them before they are lost completely. You will learn strategies for trading full gaps, partial gaps and everything in between. Then you will learn all about reversals and how to put them to use for you. You will learn how to expertly identify a reversal and how to take what you have found and profit from it via a variety of different patterns and strategies.

Finally, you will learn all about wedge patterns and how to put them to work for you. You will learn about rising, falling and sideways wedges, what each means and the strategy that will work best in each situation. When you are finished you won't be able to look at a chart without seeing something that you can make a profit from.

There are plenty of books on this subject on the market, thanks again for choosing this one! Every effort was made to ensure it is full of as much useful information as possible, please enjoy!

CHAPTER 1: MOMENTUM TRADING STRATEGY

Simply put, momentum is what day trading is all about. This is because the only way you are ever going to find a profit while day trading is by finding the stocks that are moving the most in any given day. Luckily, each day, it is not unrealistic to assume that you will be able to find at least one stock that will move as much as 30 percent. The stocks that makes these types of moves tend to all share a few common technical indicators.

Anatomy of momentum stocks

High momentum stocks will all typically share several things in common, so much so that, when given a list of 5,000 stocks, you can typically narrow the list down to 10 or less per day.

Float: First and foremost, you are going to want to look for those that have a float of less than 100mil shares. Float refers to the total number of shares that are currently available. Float can be determined by taking the total number of outstanding shares and subtracting from it the number of shares that are currently closely-held as well as those shares that are restricted. Shares that are closely-held are those that are owned by employees, major shareholders and insiders. Restricted stock shares are those that are held by insiders and are currently under a lock-up period or other temporary restriction. The smaller the float, the more volatile the stock is likely to be. Small float also indicates low liquidity and a greater ask-bid spread.

Strong daily charts: It is important that the stocks you chose are consistently above their moving averages and are trending well away from any potential support or resistance depending on if you are following an upward or a downward trend.

Substantial Relative Volume: Ideally, you will want to be on the lookout for stocks that are at least twice what the current average is. The average you are comparing to will be the current volume versus the historical average for the stock in question. Standard volume resets every night at midnight so this is a great indicator for which stocks are seeing the most action in the moment.

Fundamental catalyst: While not required, you may also find it helpful to choose stocks that are currently gaining a momentum boost from external sources. Things like activist investors, FDA announcements, aggressive public relations campaigns and earnings reports are all likely to jumpstart momentum.

Strong exit indicators

In addition to knowing what a viable stock to trade based on momentum looks like, is also important to know when you are going to want to get out to ensure you don't lose the profit you have made. Keep the following in mind and you will be able to hold onto all your hard work more reliably.

When you hit your profit target: If you hit the profit target you were aiming for them the best choice is to sell off half of your holdings and then adjust your stop loss to account for the potential for additional gains.

Red candles: If you haven't yet reached your profit target, if a candle closes out red then you should take this as an indicator to exit. If you have already sold off half of your holdings then you are going to want to hold through this first red candle as long as it doesn't trigger your stop loss

Extension bar: An extension bar is a candle with spike that causes dramatically increased profits. If this occurs you want to lock in your profits as quickly as possible as it is unlikely to last very long. This is your lucky day and it is important to capitalize on it.

Find the right screener

In order to use a momentum strategy successfully, you are going to need to use a reliable stock screener to find stocks that are trending towards the extreme ends of the market based on the above criteria. Screeners are an indispensable tool when it comes to narrowing down field of stocks that are right for you on any given day. The best screeners allow you to add in your own filters and then only display the stocks that meet all of the criteria determined. The following is a list of the most popular free screeners on the market today.

StockFetchter.com: StockFetcher can be a little complicated, but those who take the time to learn its ins and outs agree that it is one of the most powerful screeners on the market today. This power is due to its practically unlimited number of custom parameters and filters which allow you to create your own screens. The free version of this service will then allow you to see the top 5 stocks that match your criteria which is often enough to find a few worthwhile trades each day. There is also an upgraded version which will show you all of the available results for just $8.95 per month.

Finviz.com: Finviz offers thousands of premade filter combinations to return results on the most promising stocks for a given day. The tool is extremely easy to use as it offers three main drop-down menus, technical, descriptive and fundamental, and lets you choose one or more criteria from each. Results can then be sorted in 14 different ways to ensure you can always find the stocks you are hoping for. Be aware, however, that Finviz uses delayed data which makes it most effective for those who run their screens in the evenings in preparation for the next day's open.

Chartmill.com: Chartmill allows you to filter stocks based on standard criteria such as candlestick patterns, technical indicators, volume, price and performance. It also offers proprietary filters including things like trend intensity, squeeze plays and pocket pivots. Chartmill works via a credit system and provides each user with 6,000 credits per month free. Each scan then costs a few hundred credits which means most users can take advantage of their tools free of charge. Additional credits cost $10 per 10,000 or they have an unlimited option available for about $30 per month.

Stockrover.com: Stockrover is a useful tool if you are interested in trading in the Canadian market as well as the US market. It utilizes fundamental filters along with those that are performance and technical based. This tool allows you to track stocks that are near established highs and lows, those that are gaining momentum and even those that are currently being traded by major hedge funds. It also allows you to create custom screens and to create equations for more advanced screening. It then allows for backtesting to ensure the equations are up to snuff. Most of their options are available to free users but some features are gated behind a price tag of $250 per year.

Choosing the right filters

As a day trader, you are going to want to not only find stocks that have a high volume, but those that are currently experiencing a high degree of movement as well. In order to find the stocks that are going to see the greatest degree of movement, consider the following filters.

Constant volatility: In order to trade the most volatile stocks with the least amount of research try the following list of criteria in your favorite screener that allows for personalized screens. While more research is always better, you can even see success running this screen once a week and then trading the results for the coming week.

- show stocks where the average day range (50) is above 5%

- and price is between $10 and $100

- and average volume (30) is greater than 4000000

- and exchange is not Amex

- add column average volume (30)

181

- add column average day range (50)

This criterion will then return stocks that, over the past 50 days, have moved at least 5 percent each day. It is important to use at least 50 days, though 75 or 100 are going to produce even more reliable results. This shows that a given stock has moved a significant amount repeatedly over the past few months. The second criterion determines the amount you are willing to pay per share and can be altered based on your specific needs.

The next criterion determines the amount of volume you are looking for in a given timeframe. The example looks for volume over 4 million shares in the past 30 days. Next, this criterion eliminates leverage ETFs from the results which can be eliminated if you are interested in trading ETFs. Finally, the add column will show a list of the stocks with the largest volume and the greatest amount of movement. Selecting these columns will rank the results from lowest to highest based on the provided criteria.

Monitor daily to find the biggest moves: Alternately, you may prefer to search every day for the stocks that are likely to experience the greatest range of movement. To do so, you will want to create a new list of stocks each evening so that you are ready to go for the next morning when the market opens. This list can be made up of stocks that have a high volatility during the preceding day, either the greatest percentage of gains or losses. Adding in volume criteria will then help to make sure the results will continue to generate the kind of volume day trading requires. Useful filters for this search include an average volume of greater than 1 million, the greater the volume, the fewer results you will see.

When using this strategy, it is important to take note of the well-known stocks that are likely to see news release as these can often cause price movement that is unpredictable unless the details are already known. It is best to wait until after these releases have gone public to begin your trades as this is likely when both volatility and volume will be at their highest point. If you don't have your own, the earnings calendar found at Yahoo! Finance is a great place to start.

Intra-Day volatility monitoring: Another viable option is to do your research during the day to determine the stocks that are experiencing the highest degree of movement. Most trading platforms provide this information in real time. This makes it easy to keep abreast in changes that occur throughout the day. As an example, if a stock opens at a point down 10 percent from its previous close and stays there, then you know there isn't any trading happening there. However, if it starts at 10 percent down and keeps dropping then you can

184

start considering it for a potential trade. You may also find it useful to track stocks that are currently breaking their established resistance levels.

Find the biggest moves: In order to find the stocks that are very likely to make big moves without committing to constant research, you will want to focus on stocks that are proving to be constantly volatile. This is another scan that can be run over the weekend to prepare for the week ahead. Alternately, you can run this scan each evening and monitor the differences daily instead. Additionally, you may want to monitor volatility during the day to determine which stocks have been the most active during the current session.

Double check the details with chart patterns

After you have found a stock or 3 that your scanner of choice says is likely to move with the momentum you are looking for, the next step is to double check that information. This means you are going to want to start by reviewing its candlestick chart and try to determine the correct entry point based on the first pull back. It is common for traders to simply buy at the point of pull back which then creates an additional spike in volume which pushes the stock price up further. Finding the best entry point in real time is key to long-term success as a day trader.

Pennant: A pennant forms when there is significant movement in a given stock followed by a consolidation period which causes the pennant shape created by a pair of converging lines. A breakout is then likely to occur in the same direction as the previous movement. There will likely be significant movement at first, followed by weaker volume as the tip of the pennant forms, followed again by strong growth and additional volume after the breakout.

Cup and handle: The cup and handle pattern looks like the bowl of a cup with the ride side handle. The pattern is u-shaped, charting a series of lows for the stock while the handle also slopes slightly downward. This is a sign that volume is going to remain low overall and that the stock in question should be avoided.

Ascending triangle: This pattern typically forms during an upward trend and indicates that the current pattern is going to continue. It is a bullish pattern that says greater growth and volume are on the way. It can also be formed during a reversal, signaling the end to a downward trend.

Triple bottom: The triple bottom, named for the 3 bottoming out points of a given stock, tends to indicate that a reversal is on the way. You can tell a triple bottom by the fact that the price rebounds to the same point after each period of bottoming out. After the third period, it is likely to reverse the trend by breaking out.

Descending triangle: This is similar to the ascending triangle but is bearish rather than bullish. It indicates that the current downward trend is likely to continue. It can occasionally be seen during a reversal but is much more likely to be a continuation.

Inverse head and shoulders: The inverse head and shoulders consists of 3 low points always returning to the same higher price. The lowest point is considered the head while the shoulders are a pair of low points that are equal to one another. After the second shoulder, a breakout is likely to occur that will pick up volume as it goes.

Bullish triangle: This is a symmetrical triangle pattern that can be easily determined by a pair of trendlines that converge at a point. The lower trendline tracks support while the upper tracks resistance. Once the price breaks through the upper line then you know that a breakout has occurred that will rapidly pick up both steam and volume.

Rounded bottom: This pattern tracks a prolonged drop in price that will eventually rebound back to the point where it started. After the rebound occurs a reversal and breakout is likely to occur though it is best avoided as the new trend is likely not going to be strong enough to suit your day trading purposes.

Flag continuation: This pattern forms a rectangle with the support and resistance lines remaining parallel to one another. The slope of the parallel is likely to move counter to the original price movement. The point where the price breaks through can signal a strong indicator to buy or sell based on the direction of the breakout.

Bearish triangle: This triangular pattern is easy to identify because the support and resistance lines converge in a downward slope. The breakout point is always going to be on the support side and indicates a strong downward trend is forming that is likely to pick up volume significantly as it goes along.

Falling pennant: This pattern looks a lot like a triangle pattern except it doesn't quite come to a point. The trendlines will connect several peaks and valleys and once the breakout occurs it is likely that the price will move sharply in the direction of the breakout.

Double top: This pattern involves a pair of trendlines that are a good distance apart that track a price through a pair of significant downward movements that both return to the same high point in between. Once the price breaks through the support line then you can count on significant downward movement in the near future.

Head and shoulders (standard): This is the opposite of the inverse head and shoulders discussed above. It is created by three distinct price points, one at a higher point than the other two which all return to the same low point in the interim. The breakout will eventually come at the support line and will indicate the start of a new downward trend.

The importance of the bull flag: Of the patterns that you are likely to run across most frequently, the bull flag pattern may well be the most important. It is a flag that you are likely to run into every day and it provides the ability to enter at a low risk point on otherwise very strong stocks. With this pattern, you are going to want to look for an entry point after the first candle that creates a new high after the breakout has already occurred. To find this pattern, you simply keep an eye out for stocks that are squeezing up and forming tall candles. You then wait until these have formed 2 or 3 pullback candles.

The first candle to perform positively after this occurs is where you will enter, while placing a stop loss at the low point of the pull backs. It is important to get in quickly after the candle high point as right after this the volume typically spikes dramatically.

Other things to keep in mind

Setting stops properly: When it comes to day trading you always want to keep a 2 to 1 profit/loss ratio. As such, you are typically going to want to set a tight stop that is just below the first pullback point of the stock in question. A good profit target is typically 40 cents per share, which means that you are often going to want to set your stops 20 cents lower than your target. If the stop is greater than 20 cents then you may want to manually end the trade and come back for a second try. This is a good strategy because generating stops at greater than 20 cents means you quickly need to make $1 or more per trade which can be harder than it might first seem.

You will find that it is much easier to find success with 40 cents worth of profit as opposed to setting a stop of $1 and trying to make $2 of profit, the day trading market is simply too volatile for this to be successful in most instances. Your goal here should be to balance your level of risk across the entire time you spend trading. The easiest way to calculate the specific risk of a given trade is to determine the distance between the entry point and the stop. If you have a stop set at 20 cents and want to ensure the total risk is no greater than $500 then you will be able to worry about 2,500 shares at a time.

Ideal time to trade: While you can use momentum trades successfully at any time between 9:30 am and 4 pm, you will typically find them most successful between 9:30 am and 11:30 am. With that being said, if there is an incoming news release it will likely be worth your time to trade once it has been announced, regardless of the time of day. After 11:30 am, you will likely have the best results working from the 5-min chart exclusively. The 1-minute chart typically becomes much choppier after 11:30 am which can make it difficult to set stop losses effectively.

Analyze your results: Trading successfully in the long term is all about statistics which means you are going to want to keep an eye on your success/loss ratio every day to ensure that you are always moving in the right direction. At the end of each week you are going to want to determine your current trading metrics. If you have a month's worth of subpar metrics then you are going to want to take a serious look at

194

your trading strategy and determine what you can do to change it for the better.

CHAPTER 2: TRADING THE GAP

Gap trading strategies are a set of strictly regimented systems of trading that focus on a narrow band of criteria to determine profitable entry and exit points. Gap trading is a fairly simple process as you don't need to worry about bottoms or tops but the range as a whole. While the process is simple, the execution can be rather difficult and it is recommended that you practice before putting it to work in a big way.

A gap is the physical evidence of differing price levels between the end of the preceding day and the start of the next day. In general, the size of the gap in question can provide you with plenty of information when it comes to the strength of the gap as well as its location. When combined with additional information related to price action and technical analysis you can gain greater insight when it comes to the psychology and dynamics that caused it.

196

While trading based solely on the size of a gap can lead to a mixed bag of trade results, when used as part of a whole it can be a very helpful way to find the types of trades you are looking for as a day trader. The main types of gaps are outlined below. Keep in mind that, while the type of gap can help you learn about price dynamics, market sentiment and momentum, they are still lagging indicators. They can only be classified after the fact once the price has moved on.

Breakaway gap: This type of gap is used to describe a situation where the price of a given stock either gaps over a resistance or support level. This type of price gap often leads to breakouts and additional bullish movement.

Exhaustion gap: This scenario typically forms after a substantial trend has already occurred. It is generated when the price makes one final jump in the direction of the prevalent trend and then reverses dramatically.

Common gap: As the name indicates, a common gap is the most frequently seen gap which occurs without typically indicating much of anything when it comes to overall movement. Common gaps occur most frequently when the price of a given stock is ranging. They are typically not very large and, as such, tend to fill in quite quickly.

Continuation gap: This situation most frequently takes place in a trend that is already taking place. If it occurs during an uptrend then it indicates the trend is likely to continue as it marks the point that additional buyers jumped into the market, pushing the price to greater heights in the process. The same can be said for a downward trend and new sellers entering the market.

Full gap: This type of gap frequently occurs when the price at the open of the current day is dramatically different than that of the previous day. It occurs as a positive if a starting price of a given stock is greater than the high point that price reached sometime the day before. Likewise, a negative full gap appears if the starter price is below the lowest point from the previous trading day.

Partial gap: This type of gap occurs when there has been a moderate amount of change between the price between yesterday at close and today's open. A partial gap up occurs when the price at open is greater than yesterday's price at close, but is not greater than the previous day's high. A partial gap down occurs when the price at open is lower than yesterday's close, but not greater than yesterday's overall low.

Fills

When a gap is filled, it returns to the price point of its pre-gap self. Fills are always going to happen because the market prefers a stable state. When a gaps is filled within the same trading day as the gap came into existence this is referred to as fading. As an example, consider a company announces a positive news release at the end of a business day, causing a significant gap to form the following morning. As the day progresses, investor realize the news release was largely smoke and mirrors which would shift the stock from heavily bought to heavily sold. Once the price returns to yesterday's close level the gap is filled. Fills are manifested due to several different factors, including:

Technical resistance: When the price of give stock generates a gap, the price moves in a given direction so sharply that it doesn't create any new support or resistance. This gives it nothing to push against for future moves which means it takes less effort by the market to get things back to where they started from.

Irrational exuberance: Irrational exuberance occurs when investor enthusiasm reaches such a fevered pitch that it pushes stock prices to levels that aren't supported by any fundamentals. A historical example of irrational exuberance is the fervor in which the stock for internet companies were traded during the later 1990s. Spikes of irrational exuberance can be positive or negative and often leave significant gaps in their wake due to the speed at which buyers or sellers jump onto a given stock.

Price pattern: Price patterns will help you to classify gaps, making it easier to determine how quickly they are going to be filled in. Exhaustion gaps are the ones that are likely going to be filled in first as they always signal the end of an existing trend. Breakaway gaps and continuation gaps are likely to fill in much slower as they indicate the continuation of an existing trend.

Full gap strategies

The primary tenet of gap trading is to give the market 1 hour to establish a range in the stock price. After a full gap position has been entered into you will want to set a trailing stop that is 8 percent for long positions and 4 percent for short positions.

As an example, if you are going long on a particular gap which follows a stock that is currently trading at $100 then you would want to set a trailing stop at $92. If the price increases to $120 then you will want to increase the stop to $110.375. The stop will then keep rising as long as the price does the same. If you short a stock that is currently worth $100 then you will want to set a buy to cover at $104 so that a trend reversal would force an exit after 4 percent movement. If the price then drops down to $90 you would change the stop to a buy to cover of $93.

Full gap up long: If the opening price of a given stock opens above the previous day's high point then you are going to want to take a look at the short timeframe charts post 10 am. You will then want to set a long stop that is two ticks higher than the high point of the first hour of trading. In this instance, a tick is the spread of the bid/ask price which is typically between ¼ and 1/8 depending on the stock in question.

Full gap up short: If the stock price movement creates a gap but then fails to sustain the rise with sufficient buying power then the price of the stock in question will either drop below the price of the gap at open or level out. When this occurs, you will want to take advantage of it by setting short position entry signals. This means you will want to look at the 1-minute shortly after 10:30 am and set a short stop that is two ticks lower than the lowest point that was seen in the first trading hour.

Full gap down long: News of organizational changes, poor earnings, a news release with ill tidings and other market influences can all cause the price of a specific stock to drop dramatically at the start of the trading day. When a full gap down occurs at the open and then starts to climb dramatically from there, it is known as a "dead cat bounce". In order to take advantage of this position you are going to want to set a long stop at a point that equals two ticks more than the low of the previous day.

Full gap down short: If the opening price of a given stock is below the low then you are going to want to look to the short timeframe charts post 10 am before create a short stop that is equal to two ticks less than the lowest price point achieved during the first hour of trading.

Partial gap strategies

When it comes to trading partial gaps as opposed to full gaps, the biggest differences are the amount of potential gain when compared to the overall risk. As a general rule, a stock that presents a full gap has created enough of a change that the market will naturally desire to buy or sell it depending on the direction of the gap. Demand is going to be large enough to force a change. As such, the trend of full gaps tends to be much greater than those of partial gaps.

For partial gaps, the demand will naturally be smaller as well, which will require less price fluctuation to satisfy the demand. Partial gaps fill in more quickly as interest wains after the initial round of trade orders which causes the stock to return to the regular range. As such, in order to be successful with partial gap trades you will need to keep a closer trailing stop of around 5 or 6 percent as well as pay closer attention to the price movement.

Partial gap up long: If the opening price of a given stock is above the close from yesterday but does not quite reach its high, then you are dealing with a partial gap up. To take advantage of this fact you are going to want to look to the short timeframe charts post 10 am before setting a long stop that is roughly about 2 ticks over the high that was achieved during the first hour of the day.

Partial gap up short: In order to take advantage of a partial gap up by shorting you will want to look towards short timeframe charts post 10 am before setting a buy stop that is two ticks above the highest price that was achieved during the first trading hour of the day.

Partial gap down long: If the opening price is lower than the close of the previous day but not quite to that day's overall low, then you are going to want to look to the short timeframe charts post 10 am before setting a buy stop that is two ticks higher than the high point of the previous trading hour.

Partial gap down short: If the opening price for a given stock is below the close point of the previous day but not to that day's overall low then you will want to look to the short timeframe charts post 10 am before setting a short stop that equals approximately 2 ticks less than the low for the first hour of trading that day. If the stock doesn't meet the required level of volume in the meantime you will want to wait until the price breaks past the previous high, for longs, or low, for shorts, and then get out as soon as possible as the trend is unlikely to last.

Other gap trading methods

End of day gap trading: All of the trading strategies outlined above can be used for gap trading at the end of the day as well. You will need to use a stock scanner to determine the gapping stocks with the best potential for the best results. When you come across gapping stocks that are still increasing in volume then there is typically a good chance that the trend will continue. When a gapping stock crosses near the top of the resistance level this is often a reliable entry point. Likewise, a gapping short stock provides a viable entry point when the gap down crosses the support level.

Modified trading method: This trading method can be used with any of the gaps outlined above. The biggest difference with this method is that instead of waiting for the price of the given stock to break above the high or below the low you take an entry point that is in the midst of the rebound period. In order for this method to be successful you should only use it with stocks that have been trading at roughly twice their average volume for at least 5 days. Likewise, you need to ensure you have a fast trade execution system as stocks with heavy volume can reverse quite quickly. For this reason, mental stops, as opposed to hard stops, are recommended for the best results.

Gap and go: The gap and go strategy is an important one to master when it comes to chasing long-term success in the day trading arena. This strategy is specifically for use between 9:30 am and 10 am and is a great way to start the day with a few quick and easy trades. Many potential gap traders tend to focus on the gap between close of the previous day and today's open after things have settled down somewhat at the 10:30 am mark. The gap and go, on the other hand, focuses on taking advantage of the market forces that must be at work in order to generate differentials between close and open in the first place.

To utilize this strategy, you are going to want to determine which stocks have experienced either a gap up or a gap down between close and open. You will then want to go short or long depending, while placing stop losses slightly above or below the open as needed. You will then need to manage the position and trail the stop as needed to prevent loss. This strategy is useful first thing in the morning because you will receive practically instantaneous feedback regarding the effectiveness of your decision. If you are wrong you will know right away as your stop loss will trigger or, if you are right, you will definite positive movement on your position and possibly quite a bit of it.

In order to make the most of this strategy you will want to utilize some filters as well. As an example, a gap of just a few points is unlikely to be of much use, even if it moves in your preferred direction. On the other hand, a gap of 15 points or more has the potential to generate a realistic profit. Additionally, you are going to want to keep an eye out for gaps that form with substantial room between the next level of support or resistance as is relevant. If the gap is close to the level in question then it is unlikely to move much, however, if the distance is notable then the odds of profitable movement are even greater.

Trading these early morning gaps is a great way to take advantage of the path of least resistance. Even if they don't end up going anywhere useful on a given day they are quick and easy to set up, and always have the potential for significant profit. Just be sure to use accurate risk and trade management skills and there is no reason you shouldn't find success with them on a regular basis.

CHAPTER 3: REVERSAL DAY TRADING STRATEGY

A reversal occurs when the direction of an existing price trend rapidly changes directions abruptly to run parallel to the prevailing trend. On a price chart, reversals can be easily determined after they have hit the new point of resistance and dropped back the way they started. Reversals are also known as corrections, rallies or trend reversals.

An uptrend which is moving along with a series of higher lows and higher highs will reverse into a downtrend and start showing a series of lower lows and lower highs. The opposite can be said of an existing downtrend. Reversals typically occur most frequently in intraday trading as long timeframes tend to smooth things out overall. These types of reversals can happen as part of natural market correction but are more commonly seen as the result of news releases or other occurrences that suddenly change the evaluation of a given stock.

212

By keeping a close eye on technical indicators, successful traders can often determine when a reversal is occurring before it has fully formed. Additionally, if a stock has been reaching record highs or lows, then it is often natural to assume that a reversal is at hand. Specifically, you will find candlestick movements useful when it comes to determining these shifts as quickly as possible. While many traders content themselves with successfully calling bottoms or tops, the best reversal traders only enter the field once the top or bottom has already formed. Trading reversals successfully often means standing by as you wait for the perfect setup to unfold.

Mentally, it can be quite difficult to get into the reversal trading mindset because so many day traders are primed to make trades as quickly as possible when signals turn in their favor. Getting over this mental hump is key to successfully trading reversals in the long term.

In order to trade reversals successfully, it is important to never use pending orders when you know the price is approaching your target level. Additionally, you need to prepare yourself to miss out on a certain portion of the profits every time. This is an unavoidable part of the process and will ensure you win more than you lose in the long run. Finally, it is important to keep in mind that not every reversal is going to lead to an entry point. Watch your signals and don't be over anxious to chase a pattern that isn't actually materializing.

Basic reversal strategy

Find the right timeframe: The basis of all successful reversal trades involves taking a broad view of the day as a whole. This means the 4-hour or the daily charts. You will then want to add in the lines that really stand out or that were the origin of previous significant price movements.

Both resistance and support along with demand and supply level concepts can be useful when it comes to identify price levels that are especially high impact. It is important to keep in mind how important the right indicators are to the process as attempting reversals without them is little better than predicting standard market moves, which, in itself, is little better than simply gambling. Oftentimes this strategy will result in reversals that take place in mid-air, far away from your determined levels. These trades are going to have a low probability of success which means that trying to get into these reversals is not worth your time.

Choose the right reversal signal: Once the price has reached your desired level, it is important to be patient and then continue being patient as this step could take a while. Frequently you won't notice a clear signal at all and the price will start moving without you. This will happen and the sooner you learn to accept it the more effective of a reversal trader you will be. In fact, this is what your trading rules are for, they help you to filter out the price movements that are not going to be worth your time, leaving only those setups with the highest probabilities ready and waiting for you.

In general, the more pronounced time frame reversal signals are going to show themselves in the form of momentum divergences visible on either a MACD or RSI. They may also present themselves as a spike moving through an outer Bollinger band. A Fibonacci sequence that has been completed successfully will also show you are on the right track.

None of these are the true signal, however, so you will have to wait a little while longer before pulling the trigger. These signals tend to occur most frequently at the tops or the bottoms of the market and are then flooded by novice traders eager to jump on the emerging trend. Waiting until the reversal is already moving in your favor will always produce better results.

Look for the broken market structure: What you are waiting for is a lower timeframe entry trigger, which is without a doubt the hardest part of trading reversals successfully. While you would likely be able to turn a profit by entering earlier on certain trades, you are also more likely to lose out as well. Being patient is the best way to keep your overall win rate intact.

Once you see the right trend start to form, you are going to want to switch to a lower timeframe view. At the lower timeframe, you will then want to wait for the right entry point to be confirmed based on micro market structures.

One of these is a new set of highs and lows. Alternately, you could also keep an eye out for resistance and support level breaks or breaks in the trendline to trigger your entry point.

Making the most from the trade: Once you are in the trade you are going to want to put all of your focus onto Bollinger bands. As long as the price keeps a reasonable distance from the outer bands then the reversal is still occurring to an acceptable degree. A singular spike in the middle of the Bollinger bands will not signal an exit either, this will only occur when a close violates the middle Bollinger band. In order to ensure your results are consistent, it is important to always make the same decisions based on the available data. For example, if you used the 1-hour chart to determine your entry point then you would want to use it again to determine the best time to exit.

3 bar reversal pattern

3 bar patterns are one of the most common successful trade setups. This is caused by the fact that they are simple for novice traders to set up after they have completed their scans. This is also one of the reasons that the 3 bar reversal pattern can be difficult to use, simply because the setup can be found practically anywhere you look. In order to reduce the number of potential setups you can see in an intraday basis, you are going to want to add some extra requirements to the setup in order to filter out additional market noise.

Signals: First and foremost, you are only going to want to target stocks that are strongly trending in one direction. Second, the low (downtrend) or high (uptrend) bar needs to occur in the middle of a candlestick. Finally, the final bar needs to close either above the high of the first two candlesticks. With this standard in place it will then be painfully obvious once a given trend has reversed.

Unlike the preceding strategy, this strategy works in a variety of timeframes. As an example, assume you are working off of the 5-minute chart before detecting a stock that hit its low and then sharply reversed upwards. The third bar in the series would then close at a point that is higher than the highs of both of the other bars. While you can move forward if the close is above the high of the middle candlestick, it is better to know what the third candle is doing for added insurance.

The exit strategy for this pattern is just a simple moving average or even a price target. Just be sure you watch it closely and you should be fine. A good rule of thumb with this pattern is a 3 to 1 risk and reward ratio for the trade. Additionally, it is important to keep in mind that this strategy can generate quick returns no matter what time of day it is and in any market type.

False signals: These days, more and more day traders are trying to fake one another out when it comes to specific trades. Unfortunately, the 3 bar reversal pattern is not immune to this problem. One of the main reasons that the 3 bar reversal pattern fails is when volatility isn't high enough. If the market is exceedingly choppy, then the formation you are looking for is really going to be nothing more than a pause in the overall action.

This means it will not ultimately result in the type upswing or downswing that you are looking for. Adding in additional methods of confirmation before you choose your entry point will make it easier to avoid these false signals. If you buy into this type of trend it is important to be aware that it isn't moving as you would like and cut your losses before they get worse. The sooner you bail, the sooner you can get back to looking for a reversal that is actually profitable.

Hook reversal

A hook reversal is a candlestick pattern that materializes on the shorter timeframe charts. They can appear both on downtrends and uptrends and are useful when it comes to predicting a reversal in the current trend. This pattern appears as a candlestick with a higher low as well as a lower high when compared to the candlestick of the previous day. This is a somewhat unique pattern as the size difference between the body of the first and second bar is quite small when compared to other engulfing patterns.

When this pattern is found as part of an uptrend then the open will typically be near the previous high while the low will be near the previous low. This pattern is typically associated with other harami positions because the body of the second candle is formed inside the body of the first candle. As a signal for a reversal, this pattern's strength comes from the strength of the trend. The strong the trend, the stronger the signal given off by the pattern.

Abandoned baby

Bullish abandoned baby: This is another candlestick pattern that is useful when it comes to determining the potential for a reversal in the current trend. This pattern is formed by a trio of candlesticks with several distinctive characteristics. The first bar is going to be a red candlestick that is large and visible within a previously defined downtrend. The second bar will have an open equal to its close that gaps beneath the close of the first bar. The final bar is going to be a white candlestick that is large and opens higher than the second bar. This bar also represents changing trader sentiment.

This is a somewhat rare pattern but is reliable when it comes to predicting a change in the dominant downtrend. The accuracy of the signal is then further enhanced when combined with additional technical indicators including RSI and MACD.

Bearish abandoned baby: This candlestick pattern is useful when it comes to signaling a reversal in an existing uptrend. It is also a trio pattern and the first part is a white candlestick that is large and found within a previously defined uptrend. The second bar is the same as that found in the bullish abandoned baby. The final bar is a red candle that is large and will open beneath the second bar. It is also useful when it comes to determining current trader sentiment. As with the bullish abandoned baby, this is a rare but useful pattern. It signifies coming changes to the uptrend.

Outside reversal

This is a price chart pattern in which a stock's low and high prices for the day both exceed those of the previous trading session. This pattern is also known as a bearish engulfing pattern if the second bar is a down candlestick and a bullish engulfing pattern if the second bar is an up candlestick. This pattern is useful when it comes to identifying potential price movement and determining if it is likely to be bearish or bullish.

It occurs at the point a price bar falls outside the range of a previous price bar when its high is greater than the previous high and its low is lower than the previous low. As a general rule, if the outside reversal occurs at the level of resistance

225

then the signal is bearish and if it occurs at the support level then it is bullish.

Three stars in the south

This is a bullish 3 candle pattern that indicates a reversal is on its way. It occurs when the market is currently in a downtrend. The first candle will be black with a longer than average real body, a longer than average lower shadow and no upper shadow to speak of. The second candle will also be black with a shorter real body and a low that is above the first candle's low. The final candle will also be black and include a short body with no shadows and a close that is in the hi-lo range of the middle candle.

The theory behind this pattern states that bears will always lose momentum over time which will eventually ensure the bulls rally and reverse the existing trend. While extremely accurate when it comes to predicting reversals, it very rarely materializes on the charts. The reversals it predicts are also typically mild which means the upside will be small for those traders who bet on the decline. It is most useful as a signal to exit a currently held short position or initiate a long position for a small profit.

Buy weakness

This is a trading strategy that takes a proactive approach when it comes to closing out a short position or buying into a new long position. This is a useful strategy when the price of a given stock is currently falling but is expected to reverse quickly. The opposite of this strategy is useful when it comes to prices that are currently rising which is known as selling into strength.

As an example, consider a stock that is likely going to fall from \$5 to \$4.50 before then rising to a new point that is above \$5. You would then buy into the stock as it was weakening at a price point lower than \$5 and then wait until the trend reverses. You would then hold it long enough for the price to move above \$5 in order to turn a profit. If you were a short seller you could also buy into the weakness by simply closing out your position. This would involve purchasing the falling stock in the anticipation that the price will soon change direction and begin to rise.

It is common for many traders to wait for a confirmation of the impending change before reacting to a new trend. This strategy allows you to get in as early as possible in order to maximize your profits from the eventual movement. This strategy provides you with greater room for error but should only be utilized if you have utter confidence that the reversal is coming as otherwise it has too great of a chance to cost you money.

Risk reversal

This is a hedging strategy that involves selling a call and buying a put option. This then mitigates the risk of downward price movements that are unfavorable while limiting the total potential for profit from any upward movements that occur. If you are trading in the forex market then the risk reversal is the difference in volatility between the put and the call.

If you are short on an underlying instrument then hedging with this position involves implementing a long risk reversal via the purchase of a call option. You would then write a put option on the same underlying asset. On the other hand, if you are long on an underlying asset then you would short the risk reversal to hedge the position via the writing of a call

and the purchasing of a put option related to the same

underlying asset.

CHAPTER 4: WEDGE STRATEGY

Falling and rising wedges are a type of technical chart pattern that is useful when it comes to predicting both trend reversals as well as trend continuations. They form naturally on the chart as the market trends in a specific direction. Wedges are also known to appear near the end of both bearish and bullish trends. As such, wedges can have either reversal or continuation characteristics depending both on the direction of the trend as well as the type of wedge that forms.

Rising wedges: Rising wedge chart patterns typically develop when the price is hitting very high tops and extremely high bottoms. The bottoms tend to increase faster than the tops. This then causes the wedge to form an ascending corridor with the walls narrowing until the lines connect at an apex point. This formation really only signifies the potential for a bearish move in the future. Depending on the direction the market is currently moving in, this could be seen as either the continuation of an existing trend or the start of a reversal. Regardless, if the price is in the midst of a rising wedge then the price will likely soon break through the lower level of the figure.

The rising wedge is often considered one of the most difficult chart patterns to recognize and trade accurately. Despite the fact that it is a consolidation formation, the lack of upside momentum from each reoccurring high point provides the pattern with a bearish feel. Yet, the series of high highs and moderate lows keep it firmly in the bullish category. The final break of support will indicate the forces of supply typically win out which means the price is likely to drop. There are no truly reliable ways to determine how much of a decline to expect, so using additional technical indicators is recommended.

In order for a rising wedge to qualify as a reversal pattern, there needs to be an existing pattern for it to reverse. Sometimes the entire trend will be contained within the rising wedge and they can continue for as long as 6 months. If you find a rising wedge pattern in the short term, take a look at the long-term charts and see if what you are seeing is actually a continuation of something much larger to ensure you make the right choices.

Falling wedge: A falling wedge looks like the inverse of a rising wedge. It forms when the price is experiencing significantly lower than average highs and lower than normal lows. The tops are going to decrease at a rate that is greater than the lows. Falling wedges indicate a movement towards bullishness in the market which can either be a continuation of the trend or a reversal. Regardless, the price is likely to break through the upper line of the formation at some point soon.

Sideways wedge: A sideways wedge forms when a range that is already moving sideways begins to narrow. It contains higher lows and lower highs and its trigger line is always practically flat with very little slope to speak of. This type of wedge is a good indicator that you are going to want to buy when prices are low, sell when they are high and avoid the middle all together. It also lets you know that you will have an equal opportunity for success with both as the market currently lacks a directional bias.

This wedge tells you that the market is currently in a state of confusion and that other investors lack the confidence to go all in one way or the other. This should also let you know to expect fake breakouts as the wedge indicates a lack of a firm direction which will be born out in the overall movement the breakout experiences. As long as you stick to the basics, this type of wedge says the market is yours for the taking.

Putting wedges to work

When it comes to determining the likely breakout direction for a falling or rising wedge, it can be quite confusing as they can easily go in either direction. The way to accurately determine the answer lies in accurately interpreting the events that lead up to wedge's creation.

Trend continuation: If the trend is likely to continue in its current direction then the wedge is likely to play the role of a pattern correction on the chart you are watching. As an example, assume you are tracking a bullish trend that suddenly develops a falling wedge. In this case it can be thought of as a correction which means you would expect the price to breakout from the upside of the wedge.

The same can be said for rising wedges. The biggest difference is that a rising wedge instead of a falling wedge would appear. Ultimately the direction of the break is

235

determined by the price action. If a pair of rising wedges develop after a price increase has just occurred, then they likely represent the exhaustion of any previous bullish movement. After a pair of increases the tops of both will often look like a trend slowdown.

If a downtrend is occurring then the price is likely to increase after a falling wedge forms which means the price will decrease if a rising wedge forms. With this being the case, the rising wedge implies the continuation of a trend while the falling wedge indicates a reversal of the trend. While the roles of the pair of wedges can change, their potential and their behavior remains constant.

Resistance lines: For the upper resistance line, it takes at least 2 reaction highs to generate it properly, though 3 is even better. Each high should always be higher than the previous high for rising wedges and lower for falling wedges. The lower support line will also require two reaction lows, that are higher than the previous lows for rising wedges and lower for falling wedges. The upper and lower resistance points then converge as the pattern matures. The advances from the lows will become lower and lower for rising wedges and larger and larger for falling wedges. This will make any seeming rallies that occur increasingly unconvincing. If this occurs then the upper resistance line is likely to be unable to keep up with the lower support line which means a supply overhang is likely to form. This will lead to an increase in price.

Trend reversal: In some cases, a wedge will signal the reversal of a current pattern. In order to identify the reversal of a trend you will want to look for trends that are experiencing a slowdown of their main trend. This slowdown will typically terminate in a new wedge pattern. In these cases, it is common for both wedges to have the characteristics of a reversal. This is caused because the trend direction formations are opposites which means their moves are almost finished.

Trading falling and rising wedges

Entering the market: When it comes to entering the market, the first thing you will need to keep in mind is that each and every wedge uses a signal line. Depending on the type of wedge in question, this signal line will be either the upper (falling) or lower (rising) line of the pattern.

As an example, if you find a rising wedge then the signal line will be on the lower level that connects the bottoms of each point of the wedge. If you are dealing with a falling wedge then the line of the signal will connect the upper tops of the formation.

When you find a break in this single line then you will want to enter the market in the same direction as the break. As an example, if you are using a rising wedge then you will find the price of the stock breaking through the wedge's lover level which means you are going to want to go short. Likewise, when you see a falling wedge you will want to enter the market at the point the price breaks through the upper side of the wedge formation.

Use the correct timeframe: While occasionally the 1-hour chart can be used to accurately show the best wedges, the 4-hour and daily timeframe charts are often going to be your best bet. By staying away from the shorter timeframes, you will find that you have to deal with less intraday market noise. Additionally, you will find significantly fewer false breaks when compared to the 5 and 15-minute charts.

You may also find the greater timeframes give you more freedom overall which will translate into less frustration and anxiety which will make it easier for you to both find favorable trades and place them accurately. All together this will lead to a much smoother trading environment. As the mental aspect of day trading is 90 percent of finding success, this reduction of stress can be a real game changer.

Have realistic expectations: When it comes to trading wedges, it can be easy to overtrade, especially if you are using an extended time frame such as 4-hour or daily charts. Wedge trading is all about quality over quantity which means that you should be able to find success trading as few as 10 trades per month. Waiting for the right wedge setup to come along takes patience and if you get too anxious you will do little except hurt your overall trading percentage and cost yourself money. Instead of focusing on trading this strategy every day, focus on finding the right trades with the right risk and reward ratio to make it worth your time.

Placing a stop loss: When trading based on wedges the stop loss orders you place will need to be directly above the rising wedge or directly beneath the falling wedge. It is important that you do not place them too tightly as the action of the price movement will often violate one of the trendlines if you do. The price will then rebound swiftly but the damage will be done. You will instead want to look for a significant break in order to determine the right point to exit.

Taking profits: When it comes to determining the price target of this type of trade it is going to be equal to the wedge's size. As such, if you have a rising wedge then you can realistically expect the market to drop an amount that is equal to the size of the formation. If you see a falling wedge then the equity is likely to increase based on the size of the formation. If the trend is bullish then the price is likely to bounce from the trend. The price is also likely to start hesitating and close the rising wedge.

If the wedge is broken then the price is likely to decrease into a falling wedge. If the price touches the trend and the wedge breaks then the trend is likely going to move in a bullish direct.

CONCLUSION

Thank you for making it through to the end of *Day Trading: Strategies on How to Excel at Day Trading*, let's hope it was informative and able to provide you with all of the tools you need to achieve your day trading goals, whatever it is that they may be. Just because you've finished this book doesn't mean there is nothing left to learn on the topic, expanding your horizons is the only way to find the mastery you seek. Trading in the stock market can be a cutthroat experience and nowhere is it more cutthroat than in the world of day trading. As such, it is especially important to you continue to learn all you can and develop a ravenous need for new strategies because you can be sure that that is what your competition is doing.

Just because you are day trading, however, doesn't mean that you need to focus on constantly trading all of the time. The fact of the matter is that some days, and even some weeks, the market simply isn't going to want to cooperate. Truly successful traders learn to make the most of the good trades that come their way and not to force it on the days that absolutely nothing is happening. Forcing a trade where none exists is only going to cause you anxiety, frustration, cost you capital for trade fees and hurt your trade percentage to boot. Take advantage of the time off to clear your head and come back ready for success when the market is more agreeable. Focus on quality over quantity and you are far more likely to find the success you seek. Remember, day trading successfully is a marathon, not a sprint, slow and steady wins the race.

Sign Up & Join <u>Andrew Johnson's Mailing List!</u>

*EXCLUSIVE UPDATES

*FREE BOOKS

*NEW REALEASE ANNOUCEMENTS BEFORE ANYONE ELSE GETS THEM

*DISCOUNTS

*GIVEAWAYS

FOR NOTIFACTIONS OF MY *NEW RELEASES* :

Never miss my next **FREE PROMO,** my

next **NEW RELEASE** or a **GIVEAWAY!**

www.ingramcontent.com/pod-product-compliance
Lightning Source LLC
Chambersburg PA
CBHW071552210326
41597CB00019B/3207